Love
Gluten Free

Love
Gluten Free

MEGAN McKENNA

hamlyn

I'm dedicating this book to you Oli, you have brought so much happiness into my life since the moment we met. You're my forever person and I love being a mummy to our Landon. I love you so much. Thank you for everything.

First published in Great Britain in 2025
by Hamlyn, an imprint of
Octopus Publishing Group Ltd
Carmelite House
50 Victoria Embankment
London EC4Y 0DZ
www.octopusbooks.co.uk
www.octopusbooksusa.com

An Hachette UK Company
www.hachette.co.uk

The authorized representative in the EEA
is Hachette Ireland, 8 Castlecourt Centre,
Dublin 15, D15 XTP3, Ireland
email: info@hbgi.ie

Design and layout copyright © Octopus
Publishing Group 2025
Text copyright © Megan McKenna 2025
Photography copyright © Luke Albert 2025

Distributed in the US by
Hachette Book Group
1290 Avenue of the Americas
4th and 5th Floors
New York, NY 10104

Distributed in Canada by
Canadian Manda Group
664 Annette St.
Toronto, Ontario, Canada M6S 2C8

Megan McKenna has asserted her right
under the Copyright, Designs and Patents
Act 1988 to be identified as the author of
this work.

ISBN 978-060063-882-7

A CIP catalogue record for this book is
available from the British Library.

Printed and bound in China

10 9 8 7 6 5 4 3 2 1

Editorial Directors: Natalie Bradley,
    Kate Fox
Senior Editor: Alex Stetter
Art Directors: Jaz Bahra, Nicky Collings
Photographer: Luke Albert
Prop Stylist: Anna Wilkins
Food Stylist: Sam Dixon
Assistant Home Economists:
    Allegra D'Agostini, Lucy Turnbull,
    Eden Owen-Jones
Production Managers: Lucy Carter,
    Nic Jones

Publisher's note
Both imperial and metric measurements
have been given in all recipes. Use one set
of measurements only and not a mixture
of both.

FSC
www.fsc.org
MIX
Paper | Supporting
responsible forestry
FSC® C016973

CONTENTS

This book is strictly about love.
Sharing food with your loved ones
and enjoying the recipes together.
What more do you want in life?

———————

INTRODUCTION

Hello,

Oh wow, it's good to be back. If you've followed my life for a while, you know I spend most of my days in the kitchen, cooking the most comforting gluten-free dinners and singing country music.

My favourite thing in the world is to be at home prepping dinner to create a date night every evening for me and Oli. I also love cooking mouthwatering meals for our growing family – it doesn't even have to be anything too tricky, but serving something I've put my time and love into makes me so happy. I love our little family life. It's everything and more I ever dreamed of.

I've included my go-to dinner recipes in this book, and don't worry, I've taken note of what you guys love the most on my socials! So, they're all in here for you. For months, I've been writing things down as I cook (I'm normally a 'throw it all in' kind of girl), so it's taken quite a while to get these recipes perfect.

Being diagnosed with a wheat allergy and finding out I had coeliac disease at such a young age really affected the way I could eat when I was growing up. It still does now when I'm out or travelling. That was why I created my first GF cookbook, *Can You Make That Gluten Free?*, and now this second book, as you guys loved the first one so much! How could I not share more recipes with you? No one should ever not be able to enjoy food just because they have an allergy or an intolerance or an autoimmune disease. I wanted to bring the love of food back for anyone who has to suffer with one of these problems.

I can honestly say that I don't miss out on anything now. It's all about cooking from scratch and learning what you can and can't eat. You can create all your favourites at home. I've even added a takeout chapter in this book – and yes, it includes GF Chinese!! We need this luxury in life!

I really hope you love making the recipes in this book as much as I do. I feel so proud that this is my second cookbook, and you never know, it could continue… So get your apron on, light a few candles, pour a glass of wine or fizz and get yourself in that kitchen. Gluten-free people can eat good food too, and this book is the proof!

Megan X

CHAPTER 1:
BRUNCH

I always find breakfast quite boring, but I am a big fan of brunch. I've never been a Plain Jane kind of girl, so I've jazzed up a few of my favourite recipes to kick-start the day – I've even included my go-to Megan Breakfast (see page 28), which includes a lot of maple syrup.

————————————

Egg, spinach & feta muffins

Deffo not your usual type of muffin! These contain no flour at all – just a lovely selection of chopped veg in an egg batter, topped with feta, caramelized onions and walnuts. They're honestly an addictive snack.

MAKES 10

olive oil, for greasing and frying

8 eggs

½ teaspoon garlic granules

½ teaspoon sea salt flakes, plus extra for seasoning

1 teaspoon black pepper, plus extra for seasoning

30 g (1 oz) fresh spinach, finely chopped

2 large tomatoes, finely chopped

100 g (3½ oz) feta cheese, crumbled

1 red onion, thinly sliced

2 teaspoons brown sugar

2 tablespoons crushed walnuts

1 Preheat your oven to 190°C/170°C fan (350°F)/Gas Mark 5. Grease 10 holes of a muffin tray.

2 Break your eggs into a bowl, add your garlic granules, the measured salt and pepper, then whisk together. Stir in your spinach and tomatoes.

3 Spoon the egg mixture into your prepared tray and sprinkle your feta on top. Bake for 10 minutes.

4 In the meantime, drizzle some olive oil into a small frying pan over a medium heat. When hot, fry your onion for a few minutes, until translucent. Lower the heat, then add the brown sugar and season with extra salt and pepper. Allow to cook gently for about 10 minutes, until caramelized.

5 Remove your muffins from their tray. Spoon a little caramelized onion and some crushed walnuts on top of each one and serve straight away.

Shakshuka

I've never liked my eggs boring – this is my favourite way of eating them. This one-pan dish is so easy and so tasty. Perfect for dipping in your gluten-free sourdough bread.

SERVES 2

olive oil, for frying

1 onion, finely chopped

1 red pepper, finely chopped

1 red chilli, finely chopped

2 garlic cloves, finely chopped

1 teaspoon dried oregano

1 teaspoon dried parsley

1 teaspoon ground coriander

1 teaspoon garlic granules

1 teaspoon mild chilli powder

1 teaspoon smoked paprika

1 teaspoon brown sugar

1 x 400 g (14 oz) can of chopped tomatoes

1 teaspoon tomato ketchup

2 tablespoons tomato purée

4 eggs

100 g (3½ oz) feta cheese, crumbled

1 tablespoon chopped parsley

sea salt flakes and black pepper

4 slices of gluten-free sourdough bread, to serve

1 Heat a drizzle of olive oil in a large frying pan. Add your onion, pepper, chilli and garlic and cook for 3–4 minutes.

2 Add all your dried herbs and spices, your sugar and some salt and pepper. Stir for a few minutes. Then add your three tomato ingredients and stir over a medium heat until bubbling. Simmer for a good 10 minutes, until everything is nicely blended and soft.

3 Using the back of a large spoon, make 4 dents in the tomato mixture and crack an egg into each one. Cover the pan with a lid and simmer until the eggs are cooked. Season with salt and pepper again, then sprinkle your feta cheese and fresh parsley over the top.

4 Toast your bread and get ready to dip and enjoy.

Fluffy pancakes with bacon, berries & maple syrup

A new and improved version of my original fluffy pancakes recipe, this is a dream breakfast
– a showstopper for guests who stay over, or a romantic treat for your loved one.
What a great way to start the day!

MAKES 12 MINI PANCAKES

160 g (5¾ oz) gluten-free self-raising flour

160 g (5¾ oz) gluten-free plain flour

1 teaspoon gluten-free baking powder

2 eggs

300 ml (10 fl oz) semi-skimmed milk

2 tablespoons water

olive oil, for frying

200 g (7 oz) smoked streaky bacon

100 ml (3½ fl oz) double cream

maple syrup

3 tablespoons toasted flaked almonds

145 g (5¼ oz) mixed berries

1 Place your flours and baking powder in a large bowl. Add the eggs, milk and water and whisk together until you have a smooth batter.

2 Add a drizzle of olive oil to a non stick frying pan over a medium heat. When hot, fry your bacon for about 7 minutes, turning it once or twice, until crispy and golden. Transfer to a plate lined with kitchen paper to soak up the excess oil. Set aside.

3 Wipe the pan clean, then add another drizzle of olive oil and place over a medium heat. When hot, add 2 tablespoons of the batter, spaced apart, and swirl each into a circle using the back of the spoon. Cook for about 1½ minutes on each side, until lightly golden. Lower the heat and leave in the pan for another 30 seconds to make sure they are cooked inside. Transfer to a plate and keep warm. Repeat this step about 6 more times, until all the batter has been used up. You might need to add more oil between each batch to avoid them sticking to the pan.

4 To serve, pile your pancakes onto plates and top with your crispy bacon. Drizzle with cream and maple syrup to your liking, then sprinkle with flaked almonds and berries.

You can still be bouji at brunch if you're gluten-free! Taking that extra bit of time to plate up my morning meals makes me feel I'm eating like a queen. Just add your choice of coffee and you're sorted.

———

If you're ever in doubt...
just add maple syrup. Yes,
that means to anything and
everything at brunch time!
Thank me later...

————————————

Spicy tuna toastie

This is honestly my favourite sandwich, hands down. It tastes even better with a bag of cheese and onion crisps and a nice cup of tea. Thank me later!

SERVES 2

2 x 160 g (5¾ oz) cans of tuna

1 small red onion, finely chopped

6 slices jalapeño chilli, from a jar, finely chopped

1 teaspoon Tabasco sauce

2 teaspoons sriracha sauce

1 tablespoon tomato ketchup

115 g (4 oz) mayonnaise

4 slices of gluten-free bread (any type you like)

butter, for spreading

sea salt flakes and black pepper

1 Strain your tuna, add to a small bowl and mash it down.

2 Mix in your red onion and chilli, then add your Tabasco, sriracha, ketchup, mayo, salt and pepper. Stir well.

3 Toast and butter your bread, then fill to your liking with the tuna mixture.

Honey avocado bites

These are great for snacks or a bouji breakfast. You can't beat the sweetness
from the drizzle of honey.

SERVES 4

4 slices of gluten-free bread
(tiger bloomer and sourdough
are my favourites)

2 avocados, stoned, peeled and sliced
lengthways

1 lemon

1 teaspoon paprika

1 handful rocket

1 tablespoon honey

sea salt flakes and black pepper

chilli flakes, to serve (optional)

1 Toast your bread, then cut each slice in half, if
you like.

2 Arrange your avo slices evenly across the toast,
add a squeeze of lemon juice, then sprinkle with
your paprika. Top with the rocket, drizzle with
your honey and season with salt and pepper. Finish
with some chilli flakes, if you like a bit of heat.

Baked feta bruschetta

One thing you will learn about me in this book is that I love cheese. These bruschetta bites are not only packed with feta but full of flavour, thanks to the tomatoes and garlic. They're definitely a fancy brunch treat.

SERVES 4

200 g (7 oz) feta cheese

3 garlic cloves, peeled and kept whole

50 ml (2 fl oz) olive oil, plus extra for frying and drizzling

1 red onion, finely sliced

1 tablespoon sugar

10 cherry tomatoes, chopped

2 teaspoons balsamic vinegar

handful of basil leaves

2 thick slices gluten-free tiger bloomer or sourdough bread

balsamic glaze

2 tablespoons crispy onions (optional)

sea salt flakes and black pepper

1 Preheat your oven to 180°C/160°C fan (350°F)/Gas Mark 4.

2 Place your feta and garlic cloves in a baking dish. Drizzle with the measured olive oil and bake for 20–30 minutes, until golden.

3 Meanwhile, add a drizzle of olive oil to a frying pan over a medium heat. When hot, add your onion, sugar and a pinch of salt and cook until soft and caramelized. Set aside.

4 Combine your tomatoes in a bowl with your balsamic vinegar and a few torn basil leaves.

5 Once your feta and garlic are ready, transfer to a blender and blitz together to form a smooth paste.

6 Toast your bread until golden, not too dark. Drizzle each slice with olive oil and spread with your feta paste. Top with some of your caramelized shallots and the tomato mixture. Drizzle with balsamic glaze, add a few basil leaves and sprinkle with your salt and pepper. Finally, top with crispy onions if you want – I like the crunch.

The Megan breakfast

This, my friends, is my go-to breakfast – a potato waffle stack with cheesy eggs and syrup.
I highly recommend drizzling maple syrup over everything – yes, even the eggs.
Don't knock it till you try it!

SERVES 2

1 x 400 g (14 oz) can of baked beans

1 tablespoon gluten-free Worcestershire sauce

4 eggs

1 tomato, chopped

1 teaspoon Tabasco sauce

olive oil, for frying

150 g (5½ oz) Cheddar cheese, grated

4 basil or spinach leaves

4 ready-made potato waffles

2 handfuls rocket

2 teaspoon balsamic glaze

sea salt flakes and black pepper

maple syrup, to serve

1 Tip your beans into a pan over a medium heat, add your Worcestershire sauce and a sprinkle of black pepper. Stir now and then until nice and thick and heated through.

2 Meanwhile, crack your eggs into a bowl and whisk until light and frothy. Stir in your tomato, season well with salt and pepper, then add your Tabasco sauce.

3 Pour a drizzle of olive into a frying pan over a medium heat, add your eggs and let them sit for a few minutes. Once they start to cook, move them around with a spatula to create large scramble shapes. Cook to your liking, either soft and creamy or firm and dry.

4 Add two-thirds of your cheese and fold in gently, so the eggs don't break up too much, then add the basil or spinach leaves.

5 Toast your waffles on your toaster's highest setting, until crisp and brown. They might need to go down twice!

6 Stack 2 waffles on each plate and spoon your beans over half of each one so that part of them stays crunchy. Add your cheesy eggs and rocket alongside. Top the leaves with a drizzle of balsamic glaze, then season lightly with salt and pepper. Sprinkle the remaining cheese over the waffle and bean stack, and finally add a generous drizzle of maple syrup across the whole dish.

CHAPTER 2:
DATE NIGHT

I believe that date night shouldn't just happen once in a blue moon. I love cooking for Oli and making every meal special, so here are some of our favourite date-night recipes for you to make for your lover. I don't know what it is, but I get a real kick out of plating up these dishes beautifully and bringing the restaurant vibe into our home.

Pink sauce spaghetti with lardons & walnuts

Honestly, this is a favourite date night dish for me and Oli. It was one of the first meals I cooked for him, so it holds a special place in my heart. When it's just the two of us, we cook half the amount of pasta below, but serve it with the full quantity of sauce because we really love it. With my homemade Garlic & Parmesan Bread Bites (see page 150) alongside, it's irresistible and deffo a show-off meal for dinner parties.

SERVES 4

olive oil, for drizzling and frying

1 large onion, finely chopped

2 garlic cloves, finely chopped

1 x 400 g (14 oz) can of chopped tomatoes

2 tablespoons tomato purée

1 tablespoon dried oregano

1 teaspoon dried mixed herbs

100 g (3½ oz) Parmesan cheese, finely grated

handful of basil leaves

250 g (9 oz) mascarpone cheese

1 gluten-free chicken stock pot

15 g (½ oz) salted butter

100 g (3½ oz) walnuts, chopped

juice of ½ lemon

400 g (14 oz) gluten-free spaghetti

200 g (7 oz) smoked lardons

sea salt flakes and black pepper

balsamic glaze, to serve

1 Add a drizzle of olive oil to a large frying pan over a medium heat. When hot, fry your onion and garlic until softened and translucent, about 5 minutes.

2 Add your tomatoes and tomato purée, your dried herbs and a quarter of your Parmesan. Stir for a few minutes.

3 Tear up about 8 of your basil leaves and add to the sauce. Now add your mascarpone, stock pot and butter. Stir well, then season generously with salt and pepper. Leave to simmer for 10–15 minutes, then stir in the walnuts and add a generous squeeze of lemon.

4 Bring a large pan of salted water to the boil. Add your pasta and and a splash of olive oil, as GF pasta tends to stick together. Cook for about 10 minutes, stirring now and then. You want your pasta just cooked, not oversoft and sticky, so keep checking it.

5 Meanwhile, heat a drizzle of olive oil in a small frying pan and fry your lardons until crisp and browned.

6 Once your pasta is cooked, strain and add to your pan of sauce. Stir gently, then divide between bowls. Top with your lardons, your remaining Parmesan and a few basil leaves. Add a drizzle of balsamic glaze and serve.

Butter chicken & onion salad

I have a love for Indian food, so this is my favourite creamy curry to serve for date night. I like to serve it with rice and my Crispy Potato Salad (see opposite). They work so well together!

(see opposite)

SERVES 4

6 skinless, boneless chicken thighs, chopped

For the masala paste

4 heaped tablespoons Greek yogurt

1 teaspoon ginger paste

1 teaspoon garlic paste

2 tablespoons tandoori masala powder or tandoori curry powder

1 tablespoon lemon juice

For the butter sauce

1 heaped tablespoon ghee, plus extra for frying

1 onion, chopped

1 x 400 g (14 oz) can of chopped tomatoes

2 tablespoons tomato purée

1 gluten-free chicken stock pot

1 tablespoon chilli powder

2 teaspoons ground cumin

1 tablespoon ground coriander

1 teaspoon dried fenugreek

3 knobs of salted butter

300 ml (10 fl oz) double cream

1 teaspoon garam masala

sea salt flakes and black pepper

coriander leaves, to serve

1 pack of poppadums, to serve

For the onion salad

1 large onion, finely chopped

1 large tomato, finely chopped

¼ cucumber, finely chopped

handful of coriander leaves

1 First make the masala paste. Place the yogurt in a bowl and add your ginger and garlic pastes, the tandoori curry powder and lemon juice. Mix well, then set aside.

2 To make the sauce, melt the ghee in a frying pan over a medium heat. Add your onion and cook gently until softened but not browned, about 5 minutes.

3 Stir in the paste you made earlier, then add the tomatoes, tomato purée and chicken stock pot. Add your spices and a generous sprinkle of salt. Mix well and simmer for 10 minutes.

4 Add the sauce in batches to a blender and blitz until smooth. Set aside.

5 Melt another tablespoon of ghee in the frying pan. Add your chopped chicken thighs and season well. Cook for about 4 minutes.

6 Add your sauce and the knobs of butter. Once the butter has melted, stir in your cream and garam masala. Simmer gently for 15–20 minutes, stirring regularly.

7 In the meantime, assemble your onion salad. In a bowl, combine the chopped onion, tomato and cucumber, then top with the coriander leaves and set aside.

8 When you're ready to eat, sprinkle the chicken with some coriander leaves and serve with the onion salad and some poppadums.

Crispy potato salad

This goes great with any dish. I like it with the Butter Chicken (see opposite). Unlike other versions of smashed potatoes, in my recipe I roast them until crisp, then swirl them through a yogurt sauce that has a lovely crunchy texture.

SERVES 4

12 mini potatoes

olive oil, for drizzling

1 heaped teaspoon garlic granules

1 heaped teaspoon onion salt

For the sauce

200 ml (7 fl oz) yogurt

1 teaspoon Dijon mustard

1 garlic clove, crushed

juice of 1 lemon

¼ onion, chopped

½ red pepper, chopped

½ cucumber, chopped

1 celery stick, chopped

small handful of dill, finely chopped

sea salt flakes and black pepper

1 Preheat the oven to 180°C/160°C fan (350°F)/ Gas Mark 4.

2 Place your potatoes in a pan of boiling water and cook over a high heat until tender – about 10–15 minutes. Drain and lay them out on a large baking tray.

3 Using a masher, lightly press down the potatoes to crush them. Drizzle evenly with olive oil, then season with your garlic granules and onion salt, plus some salt and pepper. Bake for 45 minutes, or until crispy and golden brown.

4 Meanwhile, place your yogurt in a medium bowl and add your mustard, crushed garlic and lemon juice. Now add your onion, red pepper, cucumber, celery and dill and mix well.

5 Once your potatoes are nice and crispy, coat them in the sauce.

Pork fillet & parsnip two ways with an apple cider jus

This is a showstopper. The tender pork fillet and the sweetness of the parsnip contrast beautifully with the sharpness of the pickled apples, and the creamy cider jus tops it all off – it's like an explosion of flavours in your mouth. Enjoy this with a lovely glass of white wine.

SERVES 2

about 600 g (1 lb 5 oz) pork fillet

olive oil, for frying

15 g (½ oz) salted butter

4 spears of Tenderstem broccoli

For the pickled apples

50 g (2 oz) caster sugar

50 ml (2 fl oz) white wine vinegar

6 peppercorns

2 star anise

100 g (3½ oz) sea salt

3 crisp apples, such as Granny Smiths, peeled, cored and finely chopped

For the jus

olive oil, for frying

1 large onion, finely chopped

1 celery stick, finely chopped

300 ml (10 fl oz) apple cider

2 bay leaves

1 sprig of thyme

2 gluten-free chicken stock pots, dissolved in 200 ml (7 fl oz) boiling water

100 ml (3½ fl oz) double cream

sea salt flakes and black pepper

For the roast parsnips

3 large parsnips, quartered lengthways

olive oil, for drizzling

1 tablespoon runny honey

For the parsnip purée

olive oil, for drizzling

1 large parsnip, chopped

2 garlic cloves, chopped

125 ml (4 fl oz) milk

125 ml (4 fl oz) double cream

30 g (1 oz) salted butter

1 First make the pickled apples. Place your sugar, vinegar, peppercorns, star anise and salt in a large pan over a medium heat and mix until combined or until the sugar and salt have dissolved. Turn off the heat and leave to cool to room temperature.

2 Place the chopped apple in a large plastic bag, pour in the cooled vinegar mixture and seal tightly. Store in the fridge for at least an hour to pickle.

3 Meanwhile, make the jus. Add a drizzle of olive oil to a frying pan over a medium heat. When hot, fry your onion and celery for 4 minutes until slightly softened but not browned. Pour in your cider and heat for 2 minutes. Add your bay leaves, thyme and stock. Stir until bubbling, then lower the heat and season to taste with salt and pepper. Keep this mixture over a low heat while completing the recipe.

4 Preheat your oven to 180°C/160°C fan (350°F)/Gas Mark 4.

5 To make the roast parsnips, place your quartered parsnips in a roasting tray and drizzle with your olive oil and honey. Season with salt and pepper, then roast for 30 minutes.

6 Meanwhile, make the parsnip purée. Heat a drizzle of olive oil in a frying pan, then add the chopped parsnip and garlic. Fry for about 3 minutes. Pour in the milk and cream and bring to a simmer over a medium heat. Stir in the butter, season with salt, and leave this to cook gently.

7 Now start preparing the pork. Trim any fat from the fillet and season all over with salt and pepper. Add a drizzle of olive oil and the butter to a large frying pan over a high heat. When hot, add your fillet and brown it all over, basting it with the butter. Transfer to a roasting tray and place in your oven for 15 minutes. Set aside to rest for 5–10 minutes.

8 Once the parsnip simmering in the cream mixture is tender, transfer to your blender in batches and blitz until smooth. Set aside and keep warm.

9 Add a drizzle of olive oil to a frying pan over a high heat. When hot, add your broccoli and a splash of water, season with salt and cook for 4–5 minutes.

10 Strain your jus through a sieve into a clean pan. Add your double cream and bring to a simmer. Continue simmering until thick, about 5 minutes.

11 To serve, set out 2 plates and add 3 tablespoons of the parsnip purée to each one. Arrange your roasted parsnips on top. Carve the rested pork into slices about 2 cm (¾ inch) thick and place alongside the parsnips. Add 2 spears of broccoli to each plate and drizzle with your jus. For a final flourish of extra crunch and flavour, sprinkle a few pickled apple pieces across the top.

Taking that extra time to plate your
dinner up to be picture perfect
makes your food taste even better,
I swear. Especially when you're
serving it to your loved ones. I love
lighting a candle, dressing the table
and creating that restaurant feel
at home in the evenings. It makes
dinner time more special.

———————

Megan's take on marry-me chicken

You might doubt it, but this chicken is so delicious that anyone tasting it will want to marry you! This is one of my top three favourite dishes and a winner for a dinner party. Serve it with my Thyme & Garlic Skin-on Baby Roasties (see page 174).

SERVES 2 GENEROUSLY

4 skin-on bone-in chicken thighs

olive oil, for frying

1 tablespoon butter

1 large onion, finely chopped

2 large garlic cloves, crushed, or 1½ teaspoons garlic paste

2 teaspoons garlic granules

1 teaspoon dried oregano

1 teaspoon dried thyme

1 teaspoon dried basil

1 heaped tablespoon hot paprika

1 heaped tablespoon paprika

2 gluten-free beef stock cubes, dissolved in 600 ml (20 fl oz) boiling water

2 tablespoons tomato purée

200 ml (7 fl oz) double cream

100 g (3½ oz) Parmesan cheese, finely grated

2 sprigs of vine tomatoes (keep them on the sprigs)

sea salt flakes and black pepper

handful of basil, to serve

1 Season the chicken thighs with salt. Place a drizzle of olive oil in a large frying pan over a high heat. When hot, add your chicken thighs and cook, skin-side down, until the skin is crisp. Add your butter, turn the thighs and cook the underside for about 7 minutes. Set aside on a plate.

2 Lower the heat to medium and fry your onions in the fat remaining in the pan until it is softened and browned, about 5–7 minutes.

3 Add the garlic and the garlic granules, and all the dried herbs and spices.

4 Add your beef stock and cook over a high heat for 5–10 minutes, or until reduced by half.

5 Add your tomato purée, then lower the heat to medium and stir in your cream and cheese. Bring to a simmer, then add your chicken and vine tomatoes. Cover with a lid and cook for 15–20 minutes.

6 Add your basil, then plate up the chicken and top each portion with a sprig of vine tomatoes.

Stuffed Parmesan mushrooms

When I'm planning a date night menu, I always love to do an appetizer. These mushrooms are the perfect nibble to get your loved one's taste buds ready for the main dish.

olive oil, for frying

2 garlic cloves, finely chopped

1 shallot, finely chopped

60 g (2¼ oz) panko or other gluten-free breadcrumbs

6 medium closed-cup mushrooms, cap peeled and gills removed (optional); stalks finely chopped

2 tablespoons finely chopped parsley

100 g (3½ oz) cream cheese

100 g (3½ oz) Parmesan cheese, finely grated

1 tablespoon gluten-free all-purpose seasoning

1 teaspoon sea salt flakes

1 Preheat the oven to 180°C/160°C fan (350°F)/Gas Mark 4.

2 Add a drizzle of olive oil to a frying pan over a medium heat. When hot, add your garlic and shallot and fry until softened, about 7 minutes. Stir in your breadcrumbs and cook for 3 minutes, until crispy.

3 Place your chopped mushroom stalks in a bowl and add the mixture from the pan. Stir in your parsley, cream cheese and 3 tablespoons of the cheese. Add your all-purpose seasoning and salt and mix again.

4 Fill your mushroom caps with this filling and place them in a baking tray. Sprinkle with the remaining Parmesan, then bake in the oven for 25 minutes.

Room-service chicken with spinach

This is a favourite with Oli and me – it's so simple and so tasty! I like to serve it with creamy mashed potato and my super-easy gravy.

SERVES 2

2 large skinless, boneless chicken breasts, beaten flat (about 1 cm/ ½ inch thick) (see tip, page 62)

olive oil

2 teaspoons black pepper

2 teaspoons sea salt flakes, plus an extra pinch

30 g (1 oz) salted butter

1 teaspoon onion granules

1 tablespoon garlic granules

250g (9 oz) fresh spinach

1 teaspoon chilli flakes

2 tablespoons gluten-free gravy granules

1 gluten-free chicken stock cube or stock pot of your choice

1 quantity Creamed Parmesan Mash, to serve (see page 50)

1 Drizzle your chicken breasts with a little olive oil and season with the black pepper and sea salt.

2 Melt your butter in a large frying pan over a medium–high heat. Swirl it around, then fry your chicken breasts for about 5 minutes on each side. Baste with the butter as they cook. Transfer to a plate, sprinkle with your onion and garlic granules and keep warm.

3 Add your spinach, chilli flakes and a pinch of salt to the butter left in the pan and fry until the leaves have wilted. Set aside.

4 Place your gravy granules in a heatproof jug, add 400ml (14 fl oz) boiling water and stir to dissolve. Now add your stock and stir again to combine. This is my quick and easy way to make gravy taste extra good.

5 Serve the spinach spooned over a big dollop of my creamy mash, and sit the chicken on top. Drizzle it with any remaining buttery juices and finish with a swirl of gravy.

Creamed Parmesan mash

This is a rich and cheesy side that's delicious enough to eat on its own. If you prefer a cheese-free version, just leave out the Parmesan.

SERVES 2

4 Maris Piper potatoes (about 500 g/1 lb 2 oz in total), peeled and quartered

1 heaped tablespoon salted butter

150 ml (5 fl oz) double cream

3 tablespoons finely grated Parmesan cheese

sea salt flakes and black pepper

1 Cook your potatoes in a large pan of boiling, salted water until tender, about 20 minutes. Strain and return to the pan.

2 Add your butter, cream and cheese. Season with a generous amount of salt and pepper. Using a hand blender or electric whisk, beat together until smooth. Take care not to overbeat or the potatoes will become gluey.

Short rib ragu of dreams

This dish has been so successful for me – the first time I cooked this for Oli, he was blown away. The silky rich flavours of the ragu make everyone fall madly in love.

SERVES 4

2 large or 3 medium short ribs, from the butcher

olive oil, for frying

1 tablespoon crushed garlic

2 carrots, finely chopped

1 large onion, finely chopped

2 celery sticks, finely chopped

1 x 200 g (7 oz) tube tomato purée

½ bottle red wine

1 gluten-free beef stock cube, dissolved in 600 ml (20 fl oz) boiling water

1 x 400 g (14 oz) can of chopped tomatoes

3 tablespoons cornflour or gluten-free plain flour

3 bay leaves

1 tablespoon mixed dried herbs

1 tablespoon dried oregano

400 g (14 oz) gluten-free spaghetti

sea salt flakes and black pepper

handful of flat-leaf parsley, to serve

1 Preheat the oven to 160°C/140°C fan (325°F)/ Gas Mark 3.

2 Heavily season your ribs with salt and pepper and rub into the meat.

3 Pour a drizzle of olive oil into a large frying pan over a high heat. When hot, sear your ribs for about 4 minutes on each side, until browned. Transfer to a deep oven tray.

4 Add your garlic, carrots, onion and celery to the oily frying pan. Stir over a medium heat for a few minutes, until browned.

5 Stir in your tomato purée. Pour in your red wine and let it bubble and reduce for about 5 minutes.

6 Add your beef stock, then the chopped tomatoes. Stir for a minute or so, until heated through.

7 In a small bowl, mix 2 tablespoons of your flour with 2 tablespoons of water. Add to the tomato mixture, stirring until you have a thick sauce.

8 Pour the sauce over your ribs in the oven tray, then add your herbs. Season with salt and pepper.

9 Cover the tray with foil and place in the oven for 4 hours. If the sauce does not seem thick enough, mix the remaining flour with 2 tablespoons water and stir into the tray. Return it to the oven at 200°C/180°C Fan (400°F)/Gas Mark 6 for 40 minutes, removing the foil for the last 10 minutes.

10 Using 2 forks, pull the bones out of the ribs and discard any remaining fat. Shred the meat and mix evenly through the sauce.

11 Bring a large pan of water to the boil. Add a tablespoon of olive oil, to stop the gluten-free pasta from sticking, and a teaspoon of salt to the boiling water and cook the spaghetti for 7–9 minutes or until al dente.

12 Drain the pasta, dish it up with the ragu, scatter with parsleyand enjoy.

Honey & Parmesan carrots with spicy honey dip

This is the perfect thing to serve when your guest arrives and you're having a pre-dinner drink.

SERVES 2 AS A SIDE

5 large carrots, cut into sticks about 5 cm (2 in) long

olive oil, for drizzling

2 tablespoons honey

2 teaspoons paprika

2 teaspoons garlic granules

1 teaspoon onion granules

50 g (2 oz) Parmesan cheese, finely grated

sea salt flakes and black pepper

For the dip

6 tablespoons mayonnaise

2 tablespoons honey

1 tablespoon sriracha

1 Preheat your oven to 180°C/160°C fan (350°F)/Gas Mark 4.

2 Place your carrots in a bowl, drizzle with olive oil and toss to coat. Add your honey, paprika, garlic and onion granules and toss again.

3 Put your Parmesan into a bowl and dip each carrot in it to coat evenly. Transfer the sticks to a baking tray drizzled with olive oil, spacing them apart. Drizzle a little more olive oil across the top.

4 Season with salt and pepper, then bake for 40 minutes, turning them over halfway through. You want them crisp and brown, not burnt, so keep an eye on them.

5 Meanwhile, place your dip ingredients in a bowl and stir together. Once your carrots are cooked, dip and enjoy!

Strawberry rose ice cubes

You'll need a deep ice tray to make these fancy ice cubes, and believe me, the result is worth it. They are really impressive when you have guests over, or for date night, when you want to make your cocktail or glass of champers look pretty!

MAKES 6–8 LARGE ICE CUBES OR 18–22 SMALL ONES

6 strawberries

Prosecco, or water if you prefer

1 Cut the top off your strawberries, then slice about 5mm (¼ in) thick. Arrange a few slices in a circle (a sort of rose shape) in each compartment.

2 Fill the tray with your choice of liquid and freeze it!

CHAPTER 3:
QUICK & EASY

If you are a foodie like me – and I'm guessing you are if you've bought this book – then sometimes all you want is a tasty dish, super quick, packed full of flavour in minutes. Don't worry, I promise it's not beans on toast. Just a heads up: the steak sandwich (see page 65) is the best I've ever eaten. Once you try it, there really is no going back.

Cajun-spiced chicken pasta

Here, we're adding a bit of spice to a classic Mediterranean dish. This is perfect for a mid-week meal, when you don't have a lot of time but still want something delicious. I love the creaminess of the pasta and the chicken packed full of flavour.

SERVES 2

olive oil, for frying

1 tablespoon crushed garlic

2 tablespoons butter

200 ml (7 fl oz) double cream

2 tablespoons cream cheese

1 gluten-free chicken stock pot

4 tablespoons Cajun seasoning

1 tablespoon Italian seasoning

1 tablespoon paprika

30 g (1 oz) Parmesan cheese, finely grated, plus extra to serve

2 handfuls of fresh spinach

300 g (10½ oz) gluten-free pasta

2 skinless, boneless chicken breasts, beaten flat (about 1 cm/ ½ inch thick) (see Tip below)

sea salt flakes and black pepper

1 Add a drizzle of olive oil to a frying pan over a medium heat. When hot, fry your garlic for 2 minutes.

2 Stir in your butter, double cream, cream cheese and the stock pot. Now add 2 tablespoons of the Cajun seasoning plus the Italian seasoning, paprika, Parmesan and spinach. Leave to simmer for 3 minutes.

3 Bring a pan of salted water to the boil. Add your pasta and a splash of olive oil (as GF pasta tends to stick together) and cook for about 10 minutes, until tender but still with a bite to it.

4 Add 6 tablespoons of your pasta water to the sauce.

5 Season the chicken with the remaining 2 tablespoons Cajun seasoning.

6 Add a drizzle of olive oil to a frying pan over a medium heat. When hot, fry your chicken breasts until golden, about 4–5 minutes on each side. Set aside and keep warm.

7 Drain your pasta, add to the pan of creamy sauce and stir gently to combine. Divide between 2 bowls and sit a chicken breast on top of each. Finish with extra grated Parmesan and serve.

TIP

To flatten the chicken, place it between 2 sheets of clingfilm and bash with a rolling pin or heavy-based pan.

The best steak sandwich you will ever taste

This is my go-to sandwich. Once you try it, you will never turn back to your old sandwich ways. The sweet and spicy sauce mixed with your seasoned sliced steak, onions and Parmesan are literally the best flavours when combined. You're welcome!

SERVES 2

olive oil, for frying

1 large onion, sliced into circles about 2 cm (¾ in) thick

2 tablespoons tamari (gluten-free soy sauce)

2 tablespoons gluten-free Worcestershire sauce

2 sirloin steaks, about 200 g (7 oz) each

30 g (1 oz) salted butter

juice of ½ lemon

2 gluten-free mini baguettes or paninis, split open

handful of rocket

Parmesan cheese, finely grated

sea salt flakes and black pepper

For the sauce

55 g (2 oz) mayonnaise

2 tablespoons sriracha

1 First make the sauce. Put your mayo and sriracha into a bowl and stir together until the mixture turns pink. Set aside.

2 Add a drizzle of olive oil to a large frying pan over a medium heat. When hot, lay your onion rings in it without overlapping, then drizzle with your tamari and Worcestershire sauce. Cook until soft and golden, carefully flipping them once. Season with pepper. Set aside.

3 Season your steaks generously all over with salt and pepper.

4 Add your butter to a clean frying pan over a medium heat. When the butter turns golden brown, add your steaks and cook for about

3 minutes without moving them. Turn and cook the other side in the same way. Baste the steaks with the butter as they cook.

5 Sprinkle your lemon juice over the steaks and set aside to rest for a good 7–10 minutes. Resting makes your steak tender and prevents it from bleeding when cut, so don't cut the meat before it's been rested!

6 Toast your bread and spread a nice thick layer of the pink sauce on both halves. Add a layer of rocket.

7 Slice your steaks and arrange on the rocket. Top with your onions, then add a generous grating of Parmesan. I like to grate it finely so it melts quickly into the filling.

Top tips for your steak!
Always cook on a high heat,
and always let it rest...
Season, season, season and don't
forget to squeeze that lemon!
(I learnt from the very best,
Tom Kerridge himself)

Always add olive oil to
your water when cooking
gluten-free spaghetti. It stops
it from breaking or sticking
together. And make sure you
don't overcook it – al dente is
the way forward for us
gluten-free people!

———————

Sweet chilli chicken pittas

If you are looking for something quick but satisfying, look no further! These stuffed pitta breads are very more-ish.

SERVES 2

2 skinless, boneless chicken breasts, cut into small chunks

1 teaspoon onion granules

1 teaspoon garlic granules

2 teaspoons smoked paprika

1 teaspoon cayenne pepper

1 teaspoon sea salt flakes

2 heaped tablespoons natural yogurt

1 large tablespoon mayonnaise

2 tablespoons sweet chilli sauce

1 teaspoon honey

olive oil, for frying

1 red onion, finely sliced

1 cucumber, sliced into thin sticks

large handful of crisp salad leaves or 1 small Romaine lettuce, shredded

4 pitta breads

55 g (2 oz) Parmesan cheese, finely grated

1 Preheat your oven to 180°C/160°C fan (350°F)/ Gas Mark 4.

2 Place your chicken in a large bowl. Add the onion and garlic granules, 1 teaspoon of the smoked paprika, the cayenne pepper and salt. Mix well, then set aside

3 Place the yogurt in a separate bowl, add the mayo, sweet chilli sauce and honey and stir together. Set aside.

4 Add a drizzle of olive oil to a frying pan over a medium-high heat. When hot, add your chicken and fry for 8 minutes, until cooked through. Add to your yogurt sauce and stir well.

5 Set out your red onion, cucumber and salad leaves in separate piles.

6 Heat up your pittas in the oven for 10 minutes, flipping them over halfway through.

7 Slice open your pittas and add some lettuce, red onion and a large scoop of your chilli chicken. Top with cucumber, more red onion and a light sprinkling of Parmesan.

My very own vine tomato bolognese

One of my favourite meals is a spag bol! I've added some of my own touches to this dish and I personally think this recipe takes bolognese to the next level.

SERVES 4

olive oil, for frying

1 onion, finely chopped

500 g (1 lb 2 oz) minced beef

1 x 400 g (14 oz) can of chopped tomatoes

2 tablespoons tomato purée

1 teaspoon garlic granules

1 tablespoon dried oregano

1 tablespoon dried mixed herbs

1 teaspoon dried basil

1 gluten-free beef stock pot

1 tablespoon balsamic vinegar

2 stems of vine tomatoes or cherry tomatoes, stems and leaves removed

500 g (1 lb 2 oz) gluten-free spaghetti

sea salt flakes and black pepper

Parmesan cheese, to serve

1 Drizzle some olive oil into a frying pan over a medium heat. When hot, add your onion and fry until softened, about 5 minutes. Add your beef, breaking it up with a spatula, and fry until browned, about 10 minutes.

2 Add your canned tomatoes and tomato purée. Stir together, then add your garlic granules, oregano, mixed herbs, basil, beef stock pot and balsamic vinegar. Stir again, then taste and season with salt and pepper. Add your fresh tomatoes, cover with a lid and simmer for 35 minutes.

3 When the sauce is nearly ready, bring a large pan of salted water to the boil. Add your spaghetti and a splash of olive oil (as GF pasta tends to stick together). Cook, stirring now and then, for about 10 minutes, until al dente.

4 Drain the spaghetti, divide between 4 plates or bowls and top with the bolognese sauce. Serve with freshly grated Parmesan.

My go-to spinach & apple side salad

I serve this as a side with so many of my recipes – some old ones that are long-standing favourites, and some new ones specially created for this book. The point is that this salad makes almost any dish more exciting, and the zing of lemon really lifts a rich meal.
(See photo, page 71)

SERVES 2

100 g (3½ oz) fresh spinach

1 Pink Lady apple, quartered, cored and sliced

juice of ½ lemon

55 g (2 oz) walnuts, broken into pieces

½ red or yellow pepper, chopped into squares

1 tablespoon olive oil

1 tablespoon balsamic glaze

Parmesan cheese, freshly grated (optional)

sea salt flakes and black pepper

1 Place your spinach in a large salad bowl or 2 individual bowls.

2 Put the apple in a separate bowl, add most of your lemon juice and toss to coat the slices. Add them to the spinach.

3 Sprinkle your walnuts and chopped pepper over the salad. Drizzle with your olive oil and balsamic glaze, and the remaining lemon juice.

4 Finish with a sprinkle of salt and generous amount of black pepper. Add a grating of Parmesan if you like. Toss before eating, then tuck in.

Mini heart pizzas with honey, pepperoni & whipped ricotta

Have you ever tried honey on pizza? Perfect for serving with Valentine's Day drinks, or as a romantic treat on date night, these little heart-shaped pizzas hit the spot.

SERVES 4

2 sheets of ready-rolled gluten-free puff pastry

1 x 200 g (7 oz) tube of tomato purée

2 tablespoons dried oregano

250 g (9 oz) mozzarella cheese, grated

1 x 100 g (3½ oz) pack of pizza pepperoni

100 g (3½ oz) ricotta cheese

50 ml (2 fl oz) olive oil

2 tablespoons honey

sea salt flakes

handful of basil leaves, to serve

---

1 Preheat your oven to 180°C/160°C fan (350°F)/Gas Mark 4.

2 Place your pastry on a clean work surface and spread with your tomato purée. Sprinkle with sea salt and all your oregano.

3 Using a heart-shaped cookie cutter about 7 cm (2¾ inches) wide, stamp 6 hearts out of each sheet of pastry. (If you don't have the correct shape of cutter, draw a heart on a piece of stiff card, cut it out with scissors, then place it on the pastry and cut around it with a sharp knife before you spread the tomato purée.)

4 Sprinkle some of your mozzarella on each pastry heart and arrange your pepperoni slices on top. Transfer to a baking tray and bake for 15–20 minutes, or until the pastry is golden and puffy – keep an eye on them in the oven.

5 Meanwhile, place your ricotta and olive oil in a blender and blitz together. Spoon into a piping bag fitted with a small plain nozzle, or into a small sandwich bag from which you cut off the tip of a corner.

6 Once your pizzas are cooked, pipe mini ricotta balls onto your pizzas and drizzle some honey across them all.

7 Garnish with a few torn basil leaves and a sprinkle of sea salt before serving.

Pickle cream cheese dip

If you know me, you know I love pickles, so chopping up loads of them and mixing them into a bowl full of creamy cheese and other delicious flavours is literally heaven in a dip. I like to dip my crisps in this, or you can use veggie sticks if you are being healthy.

SERVES 4

30 g (1 oz) salted butter

150 g (5½ oz) panko or other gluten-free breadcrumbs

160 g (5¾ oz) cream cheese

225 ml (8 fl oz) soured cream

1 x 530 g (18½ oz) jar gherkins, finely chopped

small handful of dill, finely chopped

juice of 1 lemon

1 teaspoon white wine vinegar

1 tablespoon garlic granules

2 teaspoons onion powder

1 teaspoon mustard powder

1 tablespoon paprika

sea salt flakes

ready salted crinkle cut crisps, to serve

1 Add your butter to a frying pan over a medium heat. When hot, add your breadcrumbs and toast them until golden. Move them around to prevent burning, then add a sprinkle of sea salt.

2 Place your cream cheese in a bowl and add your soured cream, gherkins, dill, lemon juice and vinegar. Mix together, then add your garlic granules, onion powder, mustard powder and half of your toasted breadcrumbs. Mix well.

3 Transfer the dip to a serving bowl, then sprinkle with your paprika and the remaining toasted breadcrumbs. Serve with the crisps.

CHAPTER 4:
MADE TO SHARE

I love hosting, especially for my family. There's nothing better than sitting around a table sharing stories and sharing food. I'm very lucky to have been brought up in a family of cooks. You will always find me, my mum and my sister together in the kitchen swapping tips. The boys have it good in our household, calling us their own private chefs, while my nan sits and enjoys our crazy company. In this chapter I've chosen some of our favourite dishes that are perfect to share, or to accompany some of the main meals in the book.

Pesto pasta & burrata sharing plate

I have no time for boring salads. The pasta mixed with the caramelized onions and burrata here really makes this a hearty dish, and it's also impressive enough to serve to guests! I know I have loads of favourites, but this really is my favourite salad. I like to make some Garlic & Parmesan Bread Bites (see page 150) and offer them alongside the salad for a welcome crunch.

SERVES 4

120 g (4½ oz) gluten-free pasta shapes

olive oil

2 heaped tablespoons ready-made pesto

1 x 80 g (2¾ oz) bag rocket and mixed leaf salad

2 large tomatoes, sliced

1 quantity Caramelized Onions (see page 123)

handful of basil leaves

1 x 150 g (5¾ oz) burrata cheese

balsamic glaze

sea salt flakes and black pepper

1 Bring a large pan of salted water to the boil. Add your pasta and a splash of olive oil (as gluten-free pasta tends to stick together) and cook until al dente. Start checking after 6 minutes, as small shapes can cook quickly. When ready, drain, return to the pan and stir in your pesto plus some salt and pepper. Set aside.

2 Decant your salad leaves into a sharing bowl. Add your pesto pasta, then scatter your tomatoes and caramelized onions over it. Dot with your basil leaves, then sit your burrata in the middle.

3 Dress the whole dish with olive oil and balsamic glaze, then season with salt and pepper.

All-year Christmas dinner baps

I love Christmas and I am a sucker for a Sunday roast, but sometimes I crave one in the week. That's why I've created this mid-week bap with all the trimmings – don't forget the dipping gravy.

SERVES 4–6

1 roast-in-the-bag chicken with garlic and herbs

5 Maris Piper potatoes (about 650 g/1 lb 7 oz in total), peeled and quartered

olive oil, for drizzling

1 tablespoon duck fat (optional)

1 tablespoon dried thyme

1 x 150 g (5¾ oz) packet gluten-free stuffing mix

6 Brussels sprouts, finely sliced

salted butter

4–6 gluten-free baps or soft rolls, sliced open

cranberry sauce

2 tablespoons gluten-free gravy granules

1 gluten-free chicken stock pot

sea salt flakes and black pepper

1 Preheat your oven to the temperature indicated on the chicken bag, usually 200°C/180°C fan (400°F)/Gas Mark 6. Roast your chicken for the stated time, usually about 1½ hours.

2 Put your potatoes into a pan of salted water and bring to the boil. Lower the heat and cook until tender, testing them with a fork. Strain into a colander and give them a good shake.

3 Add a drizzle of olive oil and your duck fat (if using) to a roasting tray. Heat in the oven for a few minutes, until really hot. Add your potatoes to the tray, toss to coat in the oil, then sprinkle with your thyme and season generously with salt. Roast for about 50 minutes, turning them now and then, until they're all crispy.

4 Make your stuffing according to the packet instructions, then add a few extra tablespoons of water, if needed, so it turns into a thick paste. Spread it out to a thickness of 3 cm (1¼ inches) in

a small baking tray and drizzle with olive oil. Place in the oven for about 40 minutes.

5 Add a drizzle of olive oil to a frying pan over a medium heat. When hot, add your sprouts, season with salt and pepper and fry for about 5 minutes.

6 Once your chicken is cooked, cut a corner off the bag and pour the juices into a jug. Set aside.

7 Shred and debone your chicken. Transfer the meat to a plate and add a tiny bit of the reserved juices, so it's juicy. Season with salt and pepper.

8 Butter your baps and spread with cranberry sauce. Add the crispy stuffing next, then crush your potatoes down into the bread. Add your shredded chicken and top with your fried sprouts.

9 Stir the gravy granules and stock pot into 400 ml (14 fl oz) boiling water, for the most tasty gravy! Pour into small bowls and dip your bap as you eat!

Stuffed peppers

These go really well with my Greek Sharing Salad (see page 88). And if you're going to make that – and I suggest that you do! – here's a tip: sit a whole head of garlic, with the top sliced off, on your baking tray among the onions and roast it along with the stuffed peppers. It'll come in handy for the Honey Mustard & Roasted Garlic Dressing (see page 89).

SERVES 2

1 medium onion, cut in half

3 peppers (any colour you like)

olive oil, for frying

1 teaspoon crushed garlic

1 x 400 g (14 oz) can of chopped tomatoes

1 teaspoon dried oregano

1 teaspoon paprika

85 g (3 oz) basmati rice

1 gluten-free chicken or vegetable stock pot or cube, dissolved in 100 ml (3½ fl oz) boiling water

sea salt flakes and black pepper

1   Preheat your oven to 190°C/170°C fan (375°F)/ Gas Mark 5.

2   Chop half of your onion and 1 of the peppers.

3   Add a drizzle of olive oil to a frying pan over a medium heat. When hot, fry your chopped onion and pepper for about 5 minutes, until softened. Add your garlic and fry for another minute.

4   Add your tomatoes, oregano and paprika, then sir in your rice and stock. Heat until bubbling, then lower the heat and simmer for 5–10 minutes. Season well with salt and pepper.

5   Meanwhile, cut the tops off the 2 remaining peppers and set them aside. Remove the seeds and white membrane from inside the peppers, keeping the peppers whole. Spoon the rice filling into the hollowed-out peppers and sit them on a baking tray, with the tops of the peppers alongside. Place in the oven and roast for 30 minutes.

6   Cut the remaining half of your onion into wedges, drizzle with olive oil and add them to your tray. Continue roasting all together for a further 30 minutes, or until the rice is cooked. To serve, pop the lids back on top of the stuffed peppers.

Greek sharing salad with hot honey halloumi

Served with my Stuffed Peppers (see page 86), this halloumi salad with dressing is perfect for when you have friends over for drinks. The honey-glazed halloumi complements the peppers so well.

SERVES 2

olive oil, for frying

1 x 250 g (9 oz) block of halloumi cheese, sliced about 1 cm (½ inch) thick

2 tablespoons honey

1 x 200 g (7 oz) bag of crisp salad leaves, any you like

½ cucumber, chopped

1 large tomato, chopped

Honey Mustard & Roasted Garlic Dressing (see opposite), to serve

1 Add a drizzle of olive oil to a frying pan over a medium heat. When hot, fry your halloumi for about 3 minutes on each side, until golden.

2 Add your honey and fry for a few minutes so that it caramelizes and coats the halloumi.

3 Place your salad leaves in a large sharing bowl and sprinkle with your cucumber and tomato. Arrange your honey halloumi on top, then drizzle with the dressing.

Honey mustard & and roasted garlic dressing

You need roasted garlic for this dressing – you can pop a head of garlic in the oven when you're roasting something else, like my Stuffed Peppers (see page 86), or you can use a tablespoon or two of ready-made roasted garlic purée.

SERVES 2

juice of 1 lemon

50 ml (2 fl oz) olive oil

2 tablespoons honey

½ teaspoon Dijon mustard

1 tablespoon white wine vinegar

1 whole head of garlic, top removed and roasted (see recipe introduction, page 86)

sea salt flakes and black pepper

1 Combine the lemon juice, olive oil, honey, mustard and vinegar in a small bowl.

2 Squeeze in your roasted garlic cloves and whisk together. Season with salt and pepper.

Roasted chickpeas, carrots & feta

I'm a big fan of side dishes – the more the better, to be honest. This one has a bit of everything, and I love to serve it with fish, chicken or even on its own as an appetizer.

SERVES 2–4

5 large carrots, quartered lengthways

3 tablespoons honey

olive oil, for drizzling

1 teaspoon chilli flakes

4 teaspoons smoked paprika

1 x 400 g (14 oz) can of chickpeas, drained and patted dry with kitchen paper

1 teaspoon cayenne pepper

1 teaspoon garlic granules

1 teaspoon onion granules

115 g (4 oz) Greek yogurt

100 g (3½ oz) feta cheese

1 tablespoon walnuts, crushed

2 tablespoons chopped parsley

sea salt flakes and black pepper

1   Preheat your oven to 180°C/160°C fan (350°F)/ Gas Mark 4.

2   Place your carrots in one half of a roasting tray. Drizzle with 2 tablespoons of the honey and some olive oil. Sprinkle with your chilli flakes and 3 teaspoons of the smoked paprika, and season with salt and pepper.

3   Place your chickpeas in a bowl and mix in the remaining teaspoon of smoked paprika, your cayenne pepper, garlic and onion granules, and a sprinkle of salt. Place beside your carrots in the tray. Roast for 40 minutes.

4   Spread your Greek yogurt out on a serving plate. Spoon the crispy chickpeas over it, then arrange the carrots on top and crumble over your feta. Sprinkle with your walnuts and drizzle with the remaining tablespoon of honey. Finish with your chopped parsley!

No-fish chicken Caesar salad

Caesar salad usually contains anchovies, which not everyone likes, so this is a fish-free version. Other than that, it has everything you'd expect, including a tangy dressing and crunchy home-made garlic croutons.

SERVES 4

1 roast-in-the-bag chicken

2 large Romaine lettuces, leaves separated

100 g (3½ oz) Parmesan cheese, finely grated

For the croutons

4 slices guten-free bread, cut into 1.5 cm (⅝ inch) cubes

6 tablespoons olive oil

1 tablespoon garlic granules

sea salt flakes and black pepper

For the dressing

115 g (4 oz) natural yogurt

115 g (4 oz) mayonnaise

2 garlic cloves, crushed, or 1 heaped teaspoon garlic paste

1 teaspoon Dijon mustard

1 teaspoon gluten-free Worcestershire sauce

juice of 1 lemon (about 3½ tablespoons)

1 Preheat your oven to the temperature indicated on the chicken bag, usually 200°C/180°C fan (400°F)/Gas Mark 6. When hot enough, put your chicken in the oven for the stated time, usually about 1½ hours.

2 Now make the croutons. Place your bread squares on a large, flat baking tray. Drizzle 4 tablespoons of the oil over them. Sprinkle with your garlic granules, then season with salt and pepper. Toss together so the bread is well coated.

3 Spread the bread out again and drizzle with the remaining oil. Place on a low shelf in the oven and toast for 15 minutes, or until crisp. Set aside.

4 Meanwhile, make the dressing. Put your yogurt and mayo in a bowl. Add your garlic, mustard,

Worcestershire sauce and lemon juice. Whisk with a hand blender, then set aside in the fridge.

5 Once your chicken is cooked, cut a corner off the bag, pour the juices into a jug and set aside.

6 Break down your chicken, remove the meat from the bones and chop it into 2.5 cm (1 inch) pieces. Place in a bowl and pour the reserved juices over the meat.

7 Divide the lettuce leaves between 4 serving plates and drizzle with some of the caesar dressing. Evenly divide the chicken between the 4 plates, placing it on top of the lettuce leaves.

8 Pour over the remaining dressing, then sprinkle with grated Parmesan. Top with your croutons, add some salt and pepper, and away you go!

Warm Moroccan salad

If I'm going to have a salad, I don't like it to be boring, and this one definitely isn't. All the ingredients are so delicious, especially the crunchy chickpeas and the pomegranate seeds. This salad is comforting and healthy at the same time!

SERVES 4

1 sweet potato, skin left on, cut into slices 1.5 cm (⅝ inch) thick

olive oil, for drizzling

1 x 400 g (14 oz) can of chickpeas, drained

1 teaspoon hot paprika

½ teaspoon garlic granules

leaves from 2 sprigs of mint

1 x 200 g (7 oz) bag of mixed salad leaves

85g (3 oz) pomegranate seeds

60 g (2¼ oz) shelled pistachios

200 g (7 oz) feta cheese

½ lemon

sea salt flakes and black pepper

For the dressing

50 ml (2 fl oz) olive oil

juice of 1 lemon

2 tablespoons maple syrup

½ teaspoon Dijon mustard

½ teaspoon ground cinnamon

½ teaspoon chilli powder

1 Preheat your oven to 190°C/170°C fan (375°F)/ Gas Mark 5.

2 Arrange your sweet potato slices in a roasting tray in a single layer. Drizzle with olive oil, sprinkle with salt and roast for 25 minutes.

3 Meanwhile, combine the dressing ingredients in a bowl, add some seasoning and whisk together. Set aside.

4 Heat a drizzle of olive oil in a pan over a medium-high heat. When hot, add your chickpeas. paprika and garlic granules. Stir-fry for about 5 minutes, then set aside.

5 Chop your mint leaves very finely, then chop your salad leaves too. Place in a large bowl and mix well.

6 Chop your roasted sweet potato and mix into the salad bowl. Sprinkle with your chickpeas, pomegranate seeds and pistachios. Pour over the dressing and finish with a squeeze of lemon juice.

Barbecue pulled pork with pineapple & mini tacos

Topped with the homemade guac and pineapple chunks, these mini-tacos are full of flavour.
This is the kind of food that really gets me in the mood for a margarita.

SERVES 4

1½ tablespoons Dijon mustard

1 tablespoon paprika

1 tablespoon smoked paprika

2 tablespoons brown sugar

1 tablespoon garlic granules

1 tablespoon onion granules

1.2–1.4 kg (2½–3 lb) pork shoulder joint, excess fat trimmed off

1 gluten-free chicken stock pot, dissolved in 150 ml (5 fl oz) boiling water

200 ml (7 fl oz) barbecue sauce

4 gluten-free wraps

For the toppings

3 avocados, stoned, peeled and crushed

juice of 1 lemon

1 red onion, finely chopped

1 pineapple, peeled and cut into small chunks

125 ml (4 fl oz) soured cream

handful of coriander leaves, chopped

lime wedges, to serve

sea salt flakes and black pepper

1 Preheat the oven to 160°C/140°C Fan (325°F)/Gas Mark 3.

2 Place your mustard in a bowl with your spices, sugar, garlic and onion granules and mix well. Rub this mixture all over your pork so it's fully covered.

3 Sit your pork in a deep roasting tray and pour the stock all around it. Cover the tray with foil and place in the oven for 5 hours, by which time it will be amazingly tender.

4 Take the tray out of the oven and increase the temperature to 180°C/160°C fan (350°F)/Gas Mark 4. Using 2 forks, pull your pork apart into shreds. Add your barbecue sauce, mix well and return the tray to the oven for 30 minutes.

5 Meanwhile, use a 5 cm (2 inch) cookie cutter to stamp circles out of your wraps – you should get 4–5 out of each wrap. Toast them in a dry frying pan over a low heat, to give them a bit of colour.

6 Now prepare the toppings. Place your avocado in a small bowl and add your lemon juice and red onion. Season with salt and pepper, then set aside. Place your pineapple, soured cream and coriander leaves in separate small bowls. Put your pulled pork on a serving platter.

7 Set out all the ingredients and start building your mini tacos. Start with a spoonful of the pulled pork, add some of the avocado mixture, then soured cream, pineapple and coriander leaves. Finish with an extra squeeze of lemon juice and enjoy!

CHAPTER 5:

WHO NEEDS TAKEAWAY?

Takeaways are the bane of my life. There are hardly any good, greasy takeout places that cater for coeliacs or people with allergies, so I have solved this problem by recreating my top takeout dishes. If I had known these recipes when I was younger, I would have been so happy! After years and years of not being able to enjoy this kind of food, I can now share this little bit of heaven with you all.

————————

Hoisin duck summer rolls

I can never find a hoisin duck that is gluten-free from a takeaway, so I'm so happy to be able to share this recipe with you here. I like to roll it up in summer rolls or serve it with my Egg Fried Rice and Japanese-style Pickled Chilli Cucumber (see pages 107 and 111).

SERVES 4

1 x 1.8 kg (4 lb) duck

1 tablespoon cornflour, mixed with a splash of cold water

1 packet gluten-free summer roll rice paper rounds (you'll need about 15)

4 spring onions, shredded

½ cucumber, finely sliced into matchsticks

For the marinade

1 x 210 g (7¼ oz) jar gluten-free hoisin sauce

125 ml (4 fl oz) tamari (gluten-free soy sauce)

5 tablespoons honey

3 garlic cloves, crushed, or 2 heaped teaspoons garlic paste

1 tablespoon ginger paste

1 gluten-free chicken stock pot, dissolved in 150 ml (5 fl oz) water

1 Preheat the oven to 140°C/120°C fan (275°F)/Gas Mark 1.

2 Combine all the marinade ingredients in a bowl or jug and mix well.

3 Place your duck in an ovenproof casserole dish and brush thoroughly with the marinade. Turn it breast down, pour the rest of the marinade over it and cover with a lid. Place in the oven for 6 hours.

4 Carefully transfer the duck from the casserole dish to a roasting tray, breast side up, and return it to the oven at 200°C/180°C fan (400°F)/Gas Mark 6 for 15–20 minutes so that the skin crisps up.

5 Meanwhile, place the dish containing the marinade over a medium heat. Slowly pour in some of your cornflour paste, stirring constantly until it thickens. You might need only a bit, so stop when you've got a nice thick glaze.

6 Once your duck is looking crisp, place it on a chopping board and use 2 forks to shred the meat and skin. Transfer to a platter, pour some of your glaze over it and mix well to coat. Place any remaining glaze in a bowl.

7 To make the summer rolls, fill a large bowl with water. Briefly submerge a sheet of rice paper in the water and pat it until it becomes pliable, then transfer it to a clean work surface. Top with a spoonful of shredded duck, some spring onion and some cucumber. Fold in the sides and roll everything up into a little bundle. Repeat with the remaining ingredients and enjoy!

Japanese-inspired baked potato

When I eat out, my first choice is always Japanese. At one restaurant we go to, there's a potato dish my family always order that I can't eat, so I've recreated it at home! The flavours here go really well with my Fried Cauliflower Bites and Japanese-style Pickled Chilli Cucumber (see pages 110 and 111).

SERVES 2

2 baking potatoes

olive oil, for coating

30 g (1 oz) salted butter

1 tablespoon miso paste

2 limes

2 tablespoons ginger paste

1 tablespoon garlic granules

1 green chilli, deseeded and finely sliced

sea salt flakes and black pepper

1 Preheat your oven to 200°C/180°C fan (400°F)/ Gas Mark 6.

2 Place your potatoes on 2 separate sheets of foil. Pierce holes in the potatoes with a fork, then coat them in olive oil and season with salt and pepper. Wrap your potatoes in the foil and bake for 45 minutes.

3 Open the foil so the top and sides of the potatoes are on show, then return to the oven for a further 25 minutes.

4 Meanwhile, place your butter and miso in a bowl and beat together.

5 Grate the zest from 1 lime and stir it into the butter paste.

6 Slice the remaining lime into quarters and set aside.

7 Slice into each baked potato and open out so you can fluff up the flesh inside with a fork. Divide your butter paste between the potatoes and carefully mix with the flesh. Now add your ginger paste and mix again.

8 Sprinkle the potatoes with your garlic granules, some good pinches of sea salt flakes and your sliced green chilli.

9 Serve with your lime wedges on the side, ready to squeeze over before eating!

Seaweed crispy kale

If you think you don't like kale, this way of preparing it will change your mind. I love to serve this with Chinese-inspired dishes, or my Honey & Barbecue Chicken Strips with Jalapeño Creamed Corn (see pages 132 and 138).

SERVES 4

olive oil, for frying

1 teaspoon crushed garlic

200 g (7 oz) kale, coarse ribs removed, chopped

½ teaspoon sugar

sea salt flakes and black pepper

1 Drizzle a generous amount of olive oil into a large frying pan over a medium-high heat. When hot, add your garlic and fry for about 30 seconds – be careful, because it burns quickly. Add your kale and stir-fry until it starts to soften. Cover the pan for a few minutes to make sure it all cooks evenly.

2 Add your sugar and more olive oil if needed, plus a generous seasoning of salt and pepper. Continue cooking until the kale turns crispy and a darker green. At that point, it's ready!

Egg fried rice

Egg fried rice is great served with other Chinese dishes, but also delicious just on its own.
I like to scoop it up with prawn crackers – my little guilty pleasure!

SERVES 4

olive oil, for frying

1 onion, finely chopped

1 tablespoon crushed garlic

1 tablespoon finely chopped ginger

500 g (1 lb 2 oz) bag of stir-fry vegetables, finely chopped

1 teaspoon sugar

2 x 250 g (9 oz) pouches of ready-cooked rice

4 tablespoons tamari (gluten-free soy sauce)

3 tablespoons sweet chilli sauce

1 tablespoon oyster sauce

1 teaspoon toasted sesame oil

3 tablespoons honey

4 eggs

2 spring onions, finely sliced

150 g (5½ oz) bag of crispy fried onions

sriracha, for drizzling

sea salt flakes

prawn crackers, to serve

1 Place the oil in a large frying pan or wok over a medium to high heat. When hot, add your onion, garlic and ginger and fry for 5 minutes, until softened. Add your chopped veg, along with some salt and the sugar. Stir well, then add the rice and mix again. Now add your tamari, sweet chilli sauce, oyster sauce and sesame oil, and your honey.

2 Crack your eggs into the rice, stirring constantly to cook them. Taste and adjust the seasoning if necessary.

3 Spoon the rice onto plates and sprinkle with your spring onions and crispy onions. Drizzle some sriracha across the top and tuck in!

Fried cauliflower bites

These are an extra-special treat for gluten-free eaters as we so rarely get to eat anything deep-fried. They work perfectly as appetizers, or you can pair them with any of the Japanese-inspired dishes in this chapter. See pages 108–9 for a photo.

SERVES 2-4

60 g (2¼ oz) gluten-free plain flour

1 teaspoon paprika

1 teaspoon garlic granules

1 teaspoon onion granules

125 ml (4 fl oz) water

150 g (5½ oz) panko or other gluten-free breadcrumbs

1 cauliflower, divided into florets

200 ml (7 fl oz) vegetable oil

2 tablespoons sesame seeds

4 spring onions, sliced diagonally

sea salt flakes and black pepper

For the sauce

115 g (4 oz) mayonnaise

1 tablespoon tamari (gluten-free soy sauce)

3 tablespoons pineapple juice

3 tablespoons sweet chilli sauce

1 teaspoon ginger paste

2 tablespoons sriracha

1 Place your flour in a bowl with your paprika, garlic and onion granules, and a good seasoning of salt. Add the water and whisk until you have a smooth batter.

2 Place your panko in a separate bowl and season with salt and pepper.

3 Dip each cauliflower floret first in the batter, then in the panko, ensuring they are all well coated. Set aside on a board.

4 Combine all your sauce ingredients in a bowl, then set aside.

5 Add your oil to a wok or large frying pan over a high heat. When hot, add your cauliflower florets and stir-fry until crisp and golden. Keep them moving so they don't burn.

6 Transfer the florets to a plate lined with kitchen paper to soak up any excess oil.

7 Place a small pan over a medium heat and toast your sesame seeds for a few minutes, until lightly coloured.

8 Arrange your cauliflower bites on a serving platter and drizzle the sauce over the top. Finish by sprinkling with your sesame seeds and sliced spring onions.

Japanese-style pickled chilli cucumber

You can't get a quicker side dish than this! It needs just a short salting time, and then it quickly absorbs the flavours of the spicy dressing. I like to serve this with any of my Japanese-inspired dishes. See pages 108–9 for a photo.

SERVES 4

2 cucumbers, cut into slices 1 cm (½ in) thick

1 teaspoon sesame seeds

sea salt flakes

For the dressing

1½ tablespoons gluten-free gochujang paste

1 tablespoon honey

1 tablespoon tamari (gluten-free soy sauce)

1 garlic clove, crushed, or 1 heaped teaspoon garlic paste

1 tablespoon sesame oil

1 tablespoon rice vinegar

1 Place your cucumber slices in a bowl, sprinkle with salt and set aside for half an hour

2 Combine all the dressing ingredients in another bowl and mix well. When the cucumber is ready, pour the dressing over it and stir together. Sprinkle with sesame seeds and it's ready to eat!

Char siu pork

I love experimenting with different cuisines but struggle to find gluten-free Chinese food when I'm out or travelling, so I wanted to bring a taste of that to your home. The sweet and tangy sauce really complements the tender pork fillet.

SERVES 4

2 x 450 g (1 lb) pork loin fillets

For the marinade

4 tablespoons gluten-free hoisin sauce

4 tablespoons tamari (gluten-free soy sauce)

2 tablespoons brown sugar

6 tablespoons honey

1 tablespoon garlic paste

1 tablespoon ginger paste

2 tablespoons olive oil

2 tablespoons red food colouring

1 Combine the marinade ingredients in a bowl and mix well.

2 Place the pork in a large plastic bag and add your marinade. Seal tightly, then turn and squeeze the bag to make sure the meat is all covered. Leave to marinate in the fridge, ideally overnight, but for at least 4 hours.

3 Once the meat is ready, preheat your oven to 160°C/140°C fan (325°F)/Gas Mark 3. Line a roasting tray with foil and place a rack on it. Sit the pork on the rack, reserving the marinade. Roast for 15 minutes.

4 Meanwhile, place the marinade in a large saucepan over a medium heat and bring to a simmer. Continue heating gently until it becomes syrupy and glaze-like. Set aside.

5 Remove the partly roasted pork from the oven and spoon or brush your glaze all over it, covering both sides. Roast for a further 10 minutes, then brush with the marinade again. Increase your oven temperature to 180°C/160°C fan (350°F)/Gas Mark 4 and roast for a further 5 minutes. Set aside to rest for 10 minutes before slicing.

I'm tired of being told 'We can't make that gluten-free.' We all know it can be done. Here's the proof!

————————

Some people dream of holidays and nice cars, I dream of having a gluten-free Chinese on a Saturday night, with extra duck and plum sauce.

———————

Jerk-seasoned chicken with caramelized pineapple

I love Caribbean food, so I've created my own version of a jerk-seasoned chicken, which just tastes incredible with the glazed pineapple. I like to pair this with my Sweet Potato & Cottage Cheese Bites (see opposite).

SERVES 2

2 large skinless, boneless chicken breasts

½ teaspoon dried thyme

1 teaspoon dried parsley

1 teaspoon ground cumin

1 teaspoon onion salt

1 teaspoon garlic granules

1 teaspoon chilli flakes

1 teaspoon ground allspice

½ teaspoon ground nutmeg

½ teaspoon ground cinnamon

1 teaspoon smoked paprika

olive oil, for cooking

4 round slices of pineapple

brown sugar, for sprinkling (optional)

1 tablespoon honey

sea salt flakes and black pepper

1 Place your chicken breasts between 2 sheets of clingfilm and use a rolling pin or heavy-based pan to flatten them to a thickness of 1 cm (½ inch).

2 Put all your dried herbs and spices into a bowl and mix well.

3 Uncover your chicken, season with salt and pepper, then cover with the spice mixture.

4 Pour a splash of olive oil into a large frying pan over a medium heat. When hot, fry your pineapple slices for 5 minutes on each side, until browned. Sprinkle with a little brown sugar if you want extra sweetness, and cook for a further minute. Set aside.

5 Place another large frying pan, or 2 small ones, over a medium–high heat and pour in a generous splash of oil. When hot, add your chicken breasts and cook for 5 minutes on each side, until the spices form a crust.

6 Once cooked, drizzle your honey over the chicken and cook for a further few seconds, just to warm through.

7 Serve each chicken breast with a slice of caramelized pineapple on top.

Sweet potato & cottage cheese bites

This combination of ingredients might sound strange, but it works really well. I love these sweet potato bites with my Jerk-seasoned Chicken with Caramelized Pineapple (see opposite). They're super healthy too!

SERVES 2

1 large sweet potato, sliced into discs about 15 mm (⅝ inch) thick

olive oil, for drizzling

1 tablespoon garlic granules

5 tablespoons cottage cheese

sea salt flakes and black pepper

chopped coriander leaves or parsley, to serve (optional)

1 Preheat your oven to 180°C/160°C Fan (350°F)/ Gas Mark 4.

2 Spread your sweet potato discs over a baking tray and drizzle with olive oil. Sprinkle with your garlic granules and a generous seasoning of salt and pepper. Roast for 30 minutes.

3 Transfer to a serving platter and place a spoonful of cottage cheese on each slice, sprinkling with herbs, if you like.

Big McK fries

Who doesn't love fries? These are amazing with My Famous Burger Bowls (see page 122), or even my pasta dishes! I love saucy food, and my pickle and mayo sauce really makes this into something special.

SERVES 2

350 g (12 oz) frozen curly fries

115 g (4 oz) mayonnaise

115 g (4 oz) tomato ketchup

1 teaspoon Dijon mustard

2 large gherkins, chopped

55 g (2 oz) Cheddar cheese, finely grated

sea salt flakes

1 Preheat your oven to 220°C/200°C fan (425°F)/ Gas Mark 7.

2 Spread your fries out on a baking sheet and bake for 30 minutes, or until golden and crispy.

3 Place your mayo, ketchup, mustard and gherkins in a bowl and mix well. Set aside.

4 Once your fries are ready, sprinkle with about half your cheese and watch it melt. Drizzle your sauce all over, then season with salt and top with the remaining grated cheese.

My famous burger bowls

I know we can get gluten-free buns these days, but years of not having them has made me love a burger bowl! I packed this bowl with my best burger recipe, my burger sauce, pickles and caramelized onions. It's to die for.

SERVES 4

450 g (1 lb) minced beef

1 egg

1 tablespoon dried mixed herbs

1 tablespoon chilli flakes

1 tablespoon garlic granules

1 tablespoon onion granules

olive oil, for frying

4 cheese slices

2 Romaine lettuces, shredded

2 tomatoes, sliced

115 g (4 oz) mayonnaise

115 g (4 oz) tomato ketchup

1 teaspoon Dijon mustard

4 large gherkins, chopped

1 quantity Caramelized Onions (see opposite)

40 g (1½ oz) crispy onions

sea salt flakes and black pepper

1 Place your beef in a bowl. Add your egg, mixed herbs, chilli, garlic and onion granules and a generous seasoning of salt and pepper. Mix together with your hands and shape into 4 equal patties about 3 cm (1¼ inch) thick.

2 Add a drizzle of olive oil to a large frying pan over a medium heat. When hot, fry your burgers for 7 minutes on each side. Add a cheese slice to each one for the last minute or so, covering the pan with a lid if you want the cheese to melt quicker.

3 Transfer your burgers to a chopping board and cut into 3 cm (1¼ inch) squares.

4 Place your lettuce and tomatoes in a salad bowl, then add your burger squares.

5 Combine your mayo, ketchup and mustard in a small bowl and drizzle over your burger bowl. Add your diced gherkins and a large spoonful of caramelized onions. Finish with a sprinkle of crispy onions (I order mine online).

Caramelized onions

These caramelized onions take your dishes to the next level – adding them to anything from salads to your plate of sausage and mash really elevates the flavours.

SERVES 4

olive oil, for frying

2 red onions, finely sliced

2 heaped tablespoons brown sugar

1 Add a drizzle of olive oil to a frying pan over a medium heat. When hot, add your onions and brown sugar and cook for 5 minutes, until the onions are soft.

2 Now lower the heat and cook for a further 15 minutes, until the onions are sticky and brown.

CHAPTER 6:

FEED MY
CRAVINGS

Everything in this chapter is to die for! You will not believe that these dishes are gluten-free. I'm tired of hearing that gluten-free people can only eat plain and boring food. By the time you have finished cooking the recipes from this chapter, you will realize that we can eat finger-licking, deliciously tasty food too.

Three-cheese crispy mac & cheese

This is a new and improved recipe, with three different cheeses and paprika to give it a bit of a kick. I think this goes with everything – even a roast dinner!

SERVES 4

325 g (11½ oz) gluten-free macaroni pasta

4 slices gluten-free bread, whizzed into breadcrumbs

For the sauce

300 g (10½ oz) Cheddar cheese, grated

100 g (3½ oz) Red Leicester cheese, grated

400 ml (14 fl oz) milk

2 teaspoons garlic granules, plus extra for sprinkling

1 teaspoon onion granules

2 teaspoons smoked paprika, plus extra for sprinkling

1 teaspoon hot paprika

200 g (7 oz) mozzarella cheese, grated

2 heaped tablespoons gluten-free plain flour or cornflour mixed with 50 ml (2 fl oz) cold water

sea salt flakes and black pepper

1 Preheat your oven to 180°C/160°C fan (350°F)/Gas Mark 4.

2 Bring a large pan of salted water to the boil and cook your macaroni for just 5 minutes. (It will finish cooking in the oven.)

3 Place both your grated cheeses in a separate large pan with the milk, garlic and onion granules, and both types of paprika. Add a generous seasoning of salt and pepper and stir over a medium heat until the cheese has melted and everything has combined.

4 Add your mozzarella, then stir in your flour paste, and continue stirring as the sauce gradually thickens.

5 Drain your half-cooked pasta and place in a deep baking dish. Cover with the stringy cheese sauce and give it a stir.

6 Scatter your breadcrumbs all over the pasta. Season with more salt and pepper, and finish with a sprinkle of smoked paprika and some garlic granules. Bake for 20 minutes, until the top is brown and crisp!

Honey & barbecue chicken strips

This is always a winner in my house! The chicken strips are breadcrumbed and fried so the outside is crunchy, but the inside stays really tender. Serve them with my Homemade Ranch Dip and Paprika & Garlic Wedges (see pages 134 and 145). I also like to add my Jalapeño Creamed Corn and Seaweed Crispy Kale (see pages 138 and 106) for a real spread!

SERVES 4

4 skinless, boneless chicken breasts, cut into strips about 8 cm (3 inches) long

3½ tablespoons paprika

1 tablespoon dried mixed herbs

2 teaspoons garlic granules

1 tablespoon ground white pepper

1 teaspoon onion salt

olive oil, for drizzling

2 eggs

300 ml (10 fl oz) buttermilk

115 g (4 oz) gluten-free plain flour

55 g (2 oz) cornflour

250 ml (9 fl oz) vegetable oil, for shallow-frying

35 g (1¼ oz) brown sugar

250 ml (9 fl oz) barbecue sauce

3 tablespoons honey

3 tablespoons tomato ketchup

sea salt flakes

1 Place your chicken in a bowl and add 1½ tablespoons of your paprika, the mixed herbs, garlic granules, white pepper and onion salt. Add a drizzle of olive oil and mix together so the chicken is well coated.

2 Break your eggs into another bowl, add your buttermilk and season with salt. Whisk together to combine.

3 Put your flours in a bowl, add your remaining 2 tablespoons paprika and season well with salt.

4 Now dip each strip of chicken into your buttermilk, then your seasoned flour. Transfer to a plate.

5 Add your vegetable oil to a large frying pan over a high heat. After about 5 minutes, when it's good and hot, carefully add your chicken pieces and fry until golden, about 4 minutes on each side. (Depending on the size of your pan, you might need to cook them in batches.)

6 Meanwhile, add your sugar to a clean frying pan along with your barbecue sauce, honey and ketchup. Stir over a medium heat until combined and hot.

7 Remove the chicken from the pan and drizzle over the sauce.

Homemade ranch dip

This tangy, herby dip is amazing with the Honey & Barbecue Chicken Strips
(see page 132) and with any of my salads.

SERVES 4–6

125 ml (4 fl oz) soured cream

115 g (4 oz) mayonnaise

2 tablespoons chopped chives

2 tablespoons chopped parsley

2 tablespoons chopped dill

1 garlic clove, crushed, or 1 heaped teaspoon garlic paste

250 ml (9 fl oz) buttermilk

juice of 1 lemon

sea salt flakes and black pepper

1 Place your soured cream and mayo in a bowl, then mix in your fresh herbs and garlic. Season with salt and pepper.

2 Add your buttermilk and whisk together. Finally, add your lemon juice and whisk again.

Paprika chopped potatoes

So easy, quick and tasty! These potatoes go really well with any of my chicken, steak or pasta dishes (don't worry about having carbs on carbs, sometimes you need it). See overleaf for a photo.

SERVES 2

4 potatoes, such as Maris Piper (about 500 g/1 lb 2 oz in total)

olive oil, for drizzling

2 teaspoons smoked paprika

1 teaspoon garlic granules

1 teaspoon cayenne pepper

2 teaspoons sea salt flakes

1 teaspoon black pepper

1 Preheat your oven to 180°C/160°C fan (350°F)/ Gas Mark 4.

2 Chop your potatoes into small cubes, leaving the skin on. Spread them out on a large, flat baking tray. Drizzle with your olive oil.

3 Combine all your seasonings in a small bowl, then sprinkle over the potatoes. Mix well to ensure they are all coated.

4 Roast for about 45 minutes, turning now and then, so all the corners become crisp and brown!

Chicken Kyivs

This is another one of those things I always crave when I'm out but never get to have. Just to note that you have to freeze the garlic butter for a few hours before you cook this, but it's deffo worth the wait. I like to serve this with my Honey & Parmesan Carrots and Paprika Chopped Potatoes (see pages 54 and 135).

SERVES 4

225 g (8 oz) salted butter, at room temperature

2 tablespoons crushed garlic

2 tablespoons freshly chopped parsley

4 skinless, boneless chicken breasts, beaten flat (about 1 cm/ ½ inch thick) (see tip, page 62)

115 g (4 oz) gluten-free plain flour

3 eggs

85 g (3 oz) panko or other gluten-free breadcrumbs

2 tablespoons cayenne pepper

500 ml (18 fl oz) vegetable oil

sea salt flakes and black pepper

1   Chop your butter in a bowl, then mash in your garlic and parsley. When well mixed, shape the butter back into a block and cut into 4 equal rectangles. Wrap each slice in clingfilm and freeze for a few hours.

2   When you're ready to cook, unwrap the blocks of frozen butter and place one on each piece of chicken. Tuck in the ends and sides of the meat to enclose the butter, then wrap tightly in clingfilm and place in the fridge for 30 minutes to set the shape of the Kyivs.

3   Set out 3 wide, shallow bowls. In the first mix your flour with salt and pepper; in the second add your eggs with some salt and pepper and whisk together; in the third mix your breadcrumbs and cayenne pepper with some salt and pepper.

4   Unwrap the chilled chicken parcels. Roll each one first in the flour, then the eggs, and finally the breadcrumbs, making sure they are well coated. To prevent the parcels bursting open, coat the ends a second time, dipping them just in the egg and the breadcrumbs.

5   Preheat your oven to 180°C/160°C fan (350°F)/ Gas Mark 4.

6   Pour the oil into a deep-fat fryer and heat to 160°C (325°F). Alternatively, pour the oil into a deep saucepan, filling it no more than one-third full, and heat until a cube of bread browns in 40–45 seconds. Now add your Kyivs and deep-fry for 4 minutes, turning them in the oil, until crisp and golden.

7   Transfer the Kyivs to a baking tray and finish cooking in the oven for 25 minutes.

Jalapeño Creamed Corn

I love this – it's one of my favourite side dishes.

2 tablespoons sliced jarred jalapeños

olive oil

2 x 340 g (12 oz) cans sweetcorn, drained

1 teaspoon garlic granules

200 ml (7 fl oz) double cream

4 tablespoons grated Parmesan cheese

sea salt flakes and black pepper

1 Finely chop your jarred jalapeños and set aside.

2 Place a drizzle of your olive oil in a frying pan set over a medium–high heat. When hot, add your sweet corn, the jalapeños and the garlic granules to the pan and fry for 1 minute.

3 Stir in your cream and reduce the heat to medium. Add your grated Parmesan to the pan and keep stirring for few more minutes – you want the mixture to become thicker and more gooey.

4 Season generously with salt and black pepper.

Buffalo chicken bites

When I travel to Nashville, this is always on the menu. I love dipping these buffalo bites in the blue cheese sauce, paired with some fresh celery sticks to break up that hot sauce tingle. So tasty!

SERVES 4

4 large skinless, boneless chicken breasts, cut into bite-sized pieces

4 tablespoons paprika

2 teaspoons garlic granules

1 teaspoon onion salt

½ teaspoon ground white pepper

olive oil, for coating and frying

500 ml (18 fl oz) buttermilk

3 eggs

2 teaspoons sea salt flakes, plus extra for seasoning

120 g (4¼ oz) gluten-free plain flour

60 g (2¼ oz) cornflour

250ml (9 fl oz) gluten-free hot sauce, of your choice

60 g (2¼ oz) butter

2 tablespoons finely chopped parsley

Blue Cheese Dip (see opposite), to serve

1 Place your chicken in a bowl, add 2 tablespoons of the paprika, then the garlic granules, white pepper, onion salt and a generous sprinkle of extra sea salt. Add a splash of olive oil and mix well so that everything is coated.

2 Put your buttermilk and eggs in a separate bowl with 1 teaspoon of the sea salt and whisk together.

3 Now put your flours in a third bowl with the remaining 2 tablespoons paprika and teaspoon of sea salt. Mix well.

4 Dip each piece of chicken first in the buttermilk, then in the flour mix, turning them to coat completely. Transfer to a plate. Continue to do this until all pieces are fully covered.

5 Now we're going to shallow-fry our chicken chunks. Pour 2 cm (¾ inch) olive oil into a deep frying pan and place over a high heat. Once it's sizzling hot (a cube of bread dropped into the oil browns in 40–45 seconds), add your chicken pieces – about 6 pieces at a time, so that you don't overcrowd the pan – and fry for 3–4 minutes on each side, until golden all over. Transfer to a large baking dish.

6 Place your hot sauce and butter in a small frying pan and mix until the butter has melted. Pour this over your chicken bites, then sprinkle with parsley. Serve with my blue cheese dipping sauce.

Blue cheese dip

So easy to make, this fantastic dip goes with just about everything! It's a must with my Buffalo Chicken Bites (see opposite), but also great with celery and carrot sticks, breadsticks, crisps, crackers ... you name it!

SERVES 4

150 ml (5 fl oz) soured cream
100 ml (3½ fl oz) mayonnaise

4 tablespoons chopped chives
1 large garlic clove, crushed

150 g (5½ oz) blue cheese, crumbled

1 Place your soured cream, mayo, chives and crushed garlic in a bowl. Add your crumbled blue cheese and mix well.

2 Transfer to a serving bowl and dip away!

Paprika & garlic wedges

These taste great with my Honey & Barbecue Chicken Strips on page 132! Or with any dish, to be honest.

SERVES 4

6 floury potatoes, such as Maris Piper, unpeeled

olive oil

1 tablespoon smoked paprika

1 teaspoon hot paprika

1 tablespoon garlic granules

1 tablespoon onion granules

1 teaspoon dried mixed herbs

sea salt flakes and black pepper

1 Preheat your oven to 180°C/160°C fan (350°F)/ Gas Mark 4.

2 Cut your potatoes into wedges; they don't need to be perfect. Spread them out on a roasting tray and drizzle generously with olive oil so they're well covered. Sprinkle with all your spices and herbs, then season generously with sea salt and pepper.

3 Roast for 50 minutes, turning the wedges frequently so that they cook evenly.

I love bringing that Tennessee
kitchen vibe to the UK.
I've added some of my favourite
Nashville-inspired dishes to this
book. Yes, all gluten-free!

———————

I want people to understand that you can crave beautifully cooked gluten-free food. My guests always say to me, 'Is this really gluten-free?' Because it tastes so good!

Roasted tomato & Parmesan soup

Slow-roasting the tomatoes and onions really intensifies the flavours. I like to serve this soup with my Garlic & Parmesan Bread Bites (see page 150). Yum!

SERVES 6

28 medium tomatoes, cut into chunks

10 cherry tomatoes, left whole

2 onions, chopped

1 large head of garlic, or 2 small heads, top cut off

olive oil, for drizzling

2 tablespoons balsamic vinegar

1 tablespoon dried oregano

2 teaspoons dried mixed herbs

1 teaspoon chilli flakes

1 gluten-free chicken or vegetable stock pot, dissolved in 600 ml (20 fl oz) boiling water

1 large teaspoon sugar

2 handfuls of basil leaves, plus a few extra to serve

300 ml (10 fl oz) double cream

100 g (3½ oz) Parmesan cheese, finely grated

sea salt flakes and black pepper

1 Preheat your oven to 180°C/160°C fan (350°F)/ Gas Mark 4.

2 Place your tomatoes and onions in a large roasting tray. Sit your garlic bulb(s) in the middle. Drizzle evenly with olive oil and the balsamic vinegar, then sprinkle in your oregano, mixed herbs and chilli flakes. Add a generous seasoning of salt and pepper, then place in the oven for 45 minutes.

3 Set the garlic bulb aside. Blitz the tomatoes and onions in a blender until smooth (you might have to work in batches). Separate the roasted garlic into separate cloves, then squeeze the contents of each one into the tomato mixture and blitz again. Pour the liquid into a large pan.

4 Add your stock and stir well. Now add your sugar and basil leaves and blitz with a hand blender. I also like to strain the soup to make it extra smooth, but you can leave it slightly chunky if you prefer.

5 Place the pan over a low heat and bring to a simmer. Add your cream and about a quarter of the Parmesan, then mix together and cook for 15 minutes over a medium heat.

6 Ladle the soup into bowls and top each serving with a generous sprinkle of the remaining Parmesan and a basil leaf.

Garlic & Parmesan bread bites

I like to serve these lovely crunchy bites with soup, but they could also be served with any of my pasta dishes.

SERVES 6

100 g (3½ oz) salted butter, at room temperature

4 garlic cloves, crushed

6 slices of gluten-free bread

4 tablespoons finely grated Parmesan cheese

1 Preheat your grill until hot.

2 Place the butter and garlic in a bowl and beat together.

3 Toast your bread until golden, then spread with the garlic butter. Sprinkle with the Parmesan and grill until the cheese is melted and golden. Serve with whatever you like!

Salt & chilli chips

These chips are perfect with my Cider-Battered Fish (see page 152) and peas, but I also love to serve them with my Chinese- or Japanese-inspired dishes. They're my naughty go-to!

SERVES 2–4

300 ml (10 fl oz) vegetable oil

500 g (1 lb 2 oz) uncooked frozen chips, or (if you want a healthier option) cook some oven chips

1 tablespoon paprika

2 teaspoons sugar

1 large onion, sliced

3 teaspoons crushed garlic

2 fresh chillies, finely sliced

1 teaspoon chilli flakes

sea salt flakes and black pepper

1 If using frozen chips, pour your oil into a deep-fat fryer and heat to 160°C (325°F). Alternatively, pour the oil into a deep saucepan, filling it no more than one-third full, and place over a high heat for about 5 minutes. It's ready when a single chip sizzles straight away. At this point, add the rest of your chips and cook for about 5 minutes, turning them now and then. Taste a chip to check if they're cooked – you want them to be nearly ready at this point, but not fully crisp.

2 Use a slotted spoon to transfer the chips to a bowl. Add your paprika, sugar and a good seasoning of salt and pepper. Toss to coat.

3 Add your onion to the hot oil and fry for 3 minutes, then add your garlic and chillies and fry for a further 2 minutes. Return your chips to the pan and fry for a further 4 minutes.

4 Again using a slotted spoon, transfer the chips to a bowl lined with kitchen paper and pat dry. Remove the paper, sprinkle the chips with your chilli flakes and more salt, if needed. Serve straight away!

Cider-battered fish

Cider makes a light batter that smells amazing. I like to pair this fish recipe with my Salt & Chilli Chips and my Lemon & Chilli Mushy Peas (see pages 151 and opposite). Sooooo yum!

SERVES 2

80 g (2¾ oz) cornflour

60 g (2¼ oz) gluten-free self raising flour

1 teaspoon garlic granules

1 teaspoon onion granules

2 thick, skinless fillets of white fish, such as cod or haddock

1 tablespoon gluten-free baking powder

300 ml (10 fl oz) gluten-free cider

500 ml (18 fl oz) vegetable oil

sea salt flakes and black pepper

For the tartare sauce

115 g (4 oz) mayonnaise

125 ml (4 fl oz) soured cream

1 teaspoon Dijon mustard

2 tablespoons finely chopped gherkins

1 tablespoon finely chopped capers

juice of 1 lemon

½ teaspoon sugar

1 tablespoon chopped fresh dill

1   Place your flours, garlic and onion granules in a bowl and add a good seasoning of salt. Mix well, then dip your fish fillets in to coat each piece all over. Set aside.

2   Add your baking powder and some more salt to the flour bowl, then whisk in your cider to make a smooth batter. Set aside.

3   Let's make your sauce! Add your mayo and sour cream to a clean bowl, along with your mustard, gherkins, capers, lemon juice, sugar and dill. Season with salt and pepper and stir well, then set aside.

4   Pour the oil into a deep-fat fryer and heat to 160°C (325°F). Alternatively, pour the oil into a deep saucepan, filling it no more than one-third full, and place over a high heat for about 5 minutes. It's ready when a teaspoon of batter crisps up straight away.

5   Whisk the batter again, then dip your floured fish in it to coat completely. Carefully lower each piece into the hot oil and cook for 5–6 minutes, turning with a spatula about halfway through.

6   Transfer to a plate lined with kitchen paper and pat dry. Serve with chips and mushy peas, and your tartare sauce on the side.

Lemon & chilli mushy peas

I've always loved a mushy pea! Maybe it's the Eastender in me. This is how I like to cook and eat them, with a bit of a kick. Enjoy!

SERVES 4

350 g (12 oz) frozen garden peas

40 g (1½ oz) butter

zest of 1 lemon and juice of ½

olive oil, for frying

1 large garlic clove, finely sliced

3 spring onions, finely sliced

2 red chillies {deseeded if you want less heat}, finely sliced

sea salt flakes

1 Cook 175 g (6 oz) of your peas in a pan of boiling salted water for just a few minutes, until completely defrosted. Strain, then transfer to a blender, add your butter and blitz to combine. (This can be done in the pan with a stick blender if you prefer.)

2 Add your lemon zest to the pea mixture and blend once more. Season with little sea salt and set aside.

3 Heat a splash of olive oil in a frying pan, then fry your garlic, spring onions and chillies for 3 minutes. Add the remaining frozen peas and fry until soft – about 7 minutes.

4 Add your blended peas to this mixture and stir well. Squeeze in some lemon juice, stir again and serve.

Parmesan breaded chicken with spaghetti

This chilli tomato sauce is good enough to eat on its own just with pasta, but it's even better alongside this breaded chicken.

SERVES 2

100 g (3½ oz) gluten-free plain flour

2 eggs

100 g (3½ oz) panko or other gluten-free breadcrumbs

50 g (2 oz) Parmesan cheese, finely grated, plus extra to serve

2 skinless, boneless chicken breasts, flattened to a thickness of 5 mm (¼ inch) (see tip, page 62)

vegetable oil, for frying

200 g (7 oz) gluten-free spaghetti

2 handfuls of rocket

lemon juice, to serve

For the tomato sauce

olive oil, for frying

5 large garlic cloves, finely sliced

½ red chilli, chopped

2 x 400 g (14 oz) cans of chopped tomatoes

40 g/1½ oz piece of Parmesan cheese

1 tablespoon dried oregano

5 teaspoons brown sugar

1 tablespoon salted butter

sea salt flakes and black pepper

1 Start by making your tomato sauce. Drizzle some olive oil into a saucepan over a medium heat, then add your garlic and chilli and fry for 3 minutes.

2 Add your tomatoes and the piece of Parmesan to the pan, then stir in the oregano and sugar. Season with salt and black pepper. Leave to simmer for 15 minutes, stirring occasionally.

3 Add your butter to the tomato sauce. Check the seasoning and leave to simmer for a further 10 minutes, then reduce the heat to keep the sauce warm until you're ready to serve.

4 While the sauce is simmering, set out 3 wide, shallow bowls. In the first mix your flour seasoned with salt and pepper; in the second add your eggs with some salt and pepper and beat together; in the third mix your breadcrumbs and the grated Parmesan with some salt and pepper.

5 Evenly coat each chicken piece first with the flour, then the egg, and finally the breadcrumbs.

6 Place a generous drizzle of oil in a non stick frying pan and place over a high heat. When the oil is hot, add your chicken pieces to the pan and fry for 5 minutes on each side, until nice and crisp. Remove from the pan and set aside.

7 In the meantime, bring a large pan of salted water to the boil. Add your spaghetti and a splash of olive oil. Cook, stirring now and then, for about 7–10 minutes, until al dente.

8 Drain the spaghetti and mix it into the tomato sauce, so that everything is well covered. Divide the pasta between 2 plates. Top with a handful of rocket, then sprinkle with some grated Parmesan and finish with a squeeze of lemon. Serve alongside the breaded chicken.

CHAPTER 7:

WARMS THE HEART

No matter what time of year it is, my go-to dinners are always warming comfort dishes. There is nothing better than sitting on the sofa with Oli, eating spoonfuls of stew or tucking into a steak pie together. I know you all love my roast dinners – you've clearly got great taste, ha ha! – so I've included my top three favourite roast dinner sides in this chapter for you to enjoy.

Gorgeous beef stew with dumplings

There's something comforting about a stew topped with dumplings. Long, slow cooking makes the beef beautifully tender, and the fact that we get to have GF dumplings makes me so happy.

SERVES 6

5 tablespoons gluten-free plain flour

1 kg (2 lb 4 oz) diced stewing beef

vegetable oil, for frying

1 large onion, finely chopped

4 carrots, finely chopped

4 celery sticks, finely chopped

3 rich beef stock pots, dissolved in 1 litre (35 fl oz) boiling water

2 x 400 g (14 oz) cans of chopped tomatoes

1 x 200 g (7 oz) tube of tomato purée

4 sprigs of thyme

3 bay leaves

1 heaped tablespoon dried mixed herbs

2 tablespoons gluten-free Worcestershire sauce

2 tablespoons cornflour, mixed with a little water (optional)

sea salt flakes and black pepper

mashed potatoes and greens, to serve

For the dumplings

115 g (4 oz) gluten-free self-raising flour

180 g (6¼ oz) vegetable suet

1 teaspoon dried mixed herbs

1 teaspoon garlic granules

3 tablespoons cold water

1 Preheat your oven to 140°C/120°C fan (275°F)/ Gas Mark 1.

2 Place your flour in a large bowl and season well with salt and pepper. Add your beef, toss to coat, then set aside.

3 Heat a splash of vegetable oil in a large, ovenproof casserole dish set over a medium heat. Add your onion, carrots and celery and stir-fry for 4 minutes.

4 Add your meat and fry for a further 4 minutes, stirring continuously – you don't want it to stick.

5 Stir in your stock, canned tomatoes and tomato purée. Now add your fresh and dried herbs and Worcestershire sauce. Season with salt and pepper, stir well, then cover with foil or a lid. Cook in the oven for 5 hours, stirring it every hour or so.

6 Meanwhile, make the dumplings. Place your flour and suet in a large bowl with your herbs, garlic and salt and pepper. Mix together. Add your water and mix with a wooden spoon until you have a firm-ish dough. (You might need to add a bit more water, but go carefully with it.) Roll the mixture into 6 equal balls and set aside until needed.

7 Take the casserole dish out of the oven and increase the temperature to 180°C/160°C fan (350°F)/Gas Mark 4. If you think the stew needs thickening, add the slaked cornflour and mix well.

8 Arrange your dumplings on top of the stew, then return the dish to the oven without a lid for 30 minutes. They will expand to double their size!

9 Serve with mashed potatoes and fresh greens – I like Savoy cabbage.

Creamed cabbage

I love to serve this creamed cabbage with my roast dinners. I've been dying to share this recipe with you for ages – the bacon and the cream really take cooking cabbage to another level.

SERVES 4

olive oil, for frying

6 smoked bacon rashers, finely sliced

2 garlic cloves, crushed, or
1 tablespoon garlic paste

1 Savoy cabbage, sliced into strips
1 cm (½ inch) wide

1 tablespoon onion salt

1 tablespoon dried thyme

200 ml (7 fl oz) double cream

sea salt flakes and black pepper

1 Pour a drizzle of olive oil into a deep frying pan over a medium heat. When hot, add your bacon and fry for about 5 minutes, until it crisps up.

2 Add your garlic and fry for a minute.

3 Pour another drizzle of olive oil into the pan, then add your cabbage and fry for a few minutes, until beginning to soften. Stir in your onion salt and thyme, then add a sprinkle of sea salt and a generous seasoning of black pepper.

4 Stir in half your cream, turn down the heat and cook for 10 minutes.

5 Add the rest of your cream, turn up the heat to medium and cook for a further 5–7 minutes.

Creamy chicken & leek pie

You rarely get GF pie options when you are eating out. I love creamy chicken dishes, so I wanted to pack this pie with all these yummy ingredients. And I always smother my pie in chicken gravy.

SERVES 4

olive oil, for frying

1 large onion, chopped

2 garlic cloves, crushed, or
2 teaspoons garlic paste

5 skinless, boneless chicken thighs,
chopped into 2.5 cm (1 inch) pieces

150 ml (5 fl oz) dry white wine

2 leeks, finely sliced

1 tablespoon dried thyme

2 gluten-free chicken stock pots,
dissolved in 100 ml (3½ fl oz) boiling
water

150 ml (5 fl oz) double cream

2 tablespoons cornflour, mixed with
a little cold water

gluten-free plain flour, for dusting

2 sheets ready-rolled gluten-free
puff pastry

1 egg, beaten

sea salt flakes and black pepper

1 Preheat your oven to 180°C/160°C fan (350°F)/ Gas Mark 4.

2 Add a drizzle of olive oil to a large frying pan over a medium heat. When hot, fry your onion and garlic until soft and caramelized, about 7 minutes.

3 Add your chicken, season well with salt and pepper, and cook for 5 minutes. Pour in your wine, turn up the heat and bubble for 5 minutes to burn off the alcohol.

4 Add your leeks and cook gently for 5 minutes. Stir in the thyme and some more black pepper, then add your chicken stock. Stir to combine, then add your cream and heat for about 3 minutes, until hot.

5 Stir in your cornflour paste so that the liquid thickens into a sauce. Add more cornflour paste if you want the sauce thicker, but go carefully. Season with salt and pepper.

6 Set out a rimmed pie dish. Lightly flour a work surface and roll out 1 sheet of your pastry so that it will fit the dish. Gently press it into the corners and stick the edges down with a little beaten egg. Line the pastry case with a crumpled sheet of baking paper and fill it with baking beans or dry rice. Blind bake for 15 minutes, then lift out the paper and beans and bake the pastry for a further 5 minutes. It should look dry and lightly golden.

7 Add your filling to the pastry case, then brush the rim with beaten egg. Roll out the remaining pastry sheet and use it to cover the filling, pressing it down on the eggy rim. Trim off the excess pastry. Press around the edge of the pie with a fork, then prick the surface all over so that steam can escape. Reroll the pastry offcuts and cut out leaves. Stick them to the pastry lid with beaten egg, then brush the whole surface with the remaining egg. Bake for 40 minutes, until puffed up and golden.

Steak pie

I love warming winter dinners all year round. You can't beat a rich steak pie and using this easy, ready-made gluten-free pastry is a simple hack with a delicious result. Serve this with my Thyme & Garlic Skin-on Roasties (see page 174) or Creamed Parmesan Mash (see page 50) and always remember that extra gravy.

SERVES 4

vegetable oil, for frying

1 large carrot, chopped

1 large onion, chopped

1 celery stick, chopped

4 heaped tablespoons gluten-free plain flour, plus extra for dusting

400 g (14 oz) diced stewing beef

150 ml (5 fl oz) red wine

2 tablespoons gluten-free Worcestershire sauce

2 gluten-free beef stock pots, dissolved in 400 ml (14 fl oz) boiling water

5 tablespoons tomato purée

1 heaped tablespoon dried mixed herbs

2 tablespoons cornflour, mixed with a little water (optional)

2 sheets of ready-rolled gluten-free puff pastry

1 egg, beaten

sea salt flakes and black pepper

1 Preheat your oven to 140°C/120°C Fan (275°F)/Gas Mark 1.

2 Add a splash of vegetable oil to a large flameproof casserole dish over a medium heat. When hot, fry your carrot, onion and celery until slightly softened, about 4 minutes.

3 Mix your flour and a generous seasoning of salt and pepper in a large bowl. Add your beef and toss to coat. Tip into your onion pan and fry for about 4 minutes, just to seal.

4 Pour in your red wine and bubble for 5 minutes to burn off the alcohol.

5 Now add your Worcestershire sauce, stock, tomato purée and herbs. Season again with black pepper.

6 Cover the dish with foil or a lid and place in the oven for 2½ hours. If, at the end of this time, you think the stewed beef is not thick enough, stir in the slaked cornflour.

7 Turn the oven temperature up to 180°C/160°C Fan (350°F)/Gas Mark 4.

8 Set out a large rimmed pie dish. Lightly flour a work surface and roll out 1 sheet of your puff pastry so that it will fit the dish. Gently press it

into the corners and stick the edges down with a little beaten egg. Line the pastry case with a crumpled sheet of baking paper and fill it with baking beans or dry rice. Blind bake for 15 minutes, then lift out the paper and beans and bake the pastry for a further 5 minutes. It should look dry and lightly golden.

9 Add your filling to the pastry case, then brush the rim with beaten egg. Roll out the remaining sheet of pastry and use it to cover the filling, pressing it down on the eggy rim with a fork. Trim off the excess pastry, then prick the top of the pie all over so that steam can escape while cooking. Reroll the pastry offcuts and cut out leaves or other small shapes. Stick them to the pastry lid with beaten egg, then brush the whole surface with the remaining egg. Bake for 1 hour and 15 minutes until puffed up and golden.

Leeky cauliflower cheese

This is my favourite part of a roast dinner. The name says it all – a combination of leek and cauliflower in a rich cheese sauce. Heaven on a plate, and good enough to eat on its own.

SERVES 4-6

1 cauliflower, divided into florets

olive oil, for frying

3 leeks, sliced into 2 cm (¾ inch) pieces

300 g (10½ oz) Cheddar cheese, grated, plus extra for sprinkling

300 ml (10 fl oz) semi-skimmed milk

2 teaspoons garlic granules

2 tablespoons cornflour, mixed with a little cold water

sea salt flakes and black pepper

1 Preheat your oven to 180°C/160°C fan (350°F)/ Gas Mark 4.

2 Add your cauliflower to a large pan of salted water and bring to the boil. Strain immediately.

3 Meanwhile, add a splash of olive oil to a frying pan over a medium-high heat. When hot, add your leeks and season with salt and pepper. Cook until it's a nice golden colour.

4 Place your cheese, milk and 1 teaspoon of your garlic granules in a small saucepan over a medium heat. Stir constantly until the cheese has melted. Add your cornflour and cook, still stirring, for a further few minutes to make a smooth sauce.

5 Tip your cauliflower into a small baking dish, about 20 x 20 cm (8 x 8 inches), so that it nearly reaches the rim. Spread your leeks over the top, then cover with your sauce. Sprinkle the remaining teaspoon of garlic granules and a little more cheese over the top. Bake for 40 minutes, until golden and bubbling.

Thyme & garlic skin-on roasties

I love all kinds of roast potatoes, but these are definitely my favourite right now. I would say that these are my posh roast potatoes, fluffy inside with crispy skin. They work well with any dish.

SERVES 4

1 kg (2 lb 4 oz) baby potatoes

2 tablespoons duck fat

1 tablespoon dried thyme

1 tablespoon garlic granules

sea salt flakes and black pepper

1 Preheat your oven to 180°C/160°C fan (350°F)/Gas Mark 4.

2 Add your potatoes to a pan of boiling water and cook for 15 minutes, until a fork goes in easily.

3 Place your duck fat in a roasting tray and heat in the oven for 5 minutes.

4 Strain your potatoes, then return to the pan and shake so that the edges roughen up a bit. Carefully add them to your tray of hot duck fat and turn to coat. Sprinkle with the thyme and garlic, and roast for 50 minutes, turning now and then so they colour evenly. You want them nice and crispy on the outside and fluffy in the middle!

CHAPTER 8:
SWEET TREATS

If you're anything like me, you like to finish a nice big dinner with something sweet. I always end date night with something sugary, cute and pretty.
In this chapter, I've put together some of my favourite desserts. These recipes are so delicious, you can share them with your family, loved one or just eat them all yourself.

McK apple pies

When I'm going through a certain fast-food drive-through, the apple pies always look insane, but I can never get a gluten-free alternative. So I've created my own version, so you don't have to feel like you're missing out.

MAKES 12

4 apples, peeled, cored and chopped

60 g (2¼ oz) butter

125 g (4½ oz) light brown sugar

2 teaspoons ground cinnamon

juice of ½ lemon

2 sheets ready-rolled gluten-free puff pastry

1 egg, beaten

vegetable oil, for frying

icing sugar, for dusting

1 Place the apples, butter, sugar, cinnamon and lemon juice in a pan and stir over a medium heat until the apples are soft and the liquid has evaporated, about 25 minutes. Transfer to a bowl and leave to cool.

2 Set out your pastry sheets on a clean work surface and cut each of them into 6 equal rectangles. Place 2 teaspoons of the cooled apples in the centre of each rectangle. Brush beaten egg around the edges of each one, then fold the pastry over and press down the edges with a fork. Brush the remaining beaten egg over the top of the pastries, making sure to cover both sides.

3 Pour a 2.5 cm (1 inch) depth of oil into a large pan and heat until it reaches 175°C (345°F). Add the pastries a few at a time and cook until crisp and golden brown on both sides – about 2 minutes on each side. Drain on a plate lined with kitchen paper and dust with icing sugar before serving.

Crispy marshmallow bars

This dessert is so fun to make, and I love it because it's pink! I've made this extra-special by finishing it off with chocolate, mini marshmallows and sea salt flakes – it really is an unreal snack.

30 g (1 oz) salted butter

425 g (15 oz) large marshmallows

350 g (12 oz) gluten-free rice pops

100 g (3½ oz) white chocolate chips

100 g (3½ oz) milk chocolate chips

180 g (6¼ oz) milk chocolate, broken into pieces

100 g (3½ oz) mini marshmallows

½ teaspoon sea salt flakes

1 Place your butter in a pan over a medium heat and allow to melt.

2 Lower the heat, then add your large marshmallows to the pan and stir until a thick but pourable paste forms, about 5–7 minutes.

3 Take the pan off the heat, then add your rice pops and mix well. Now stir in the white and milk chocolate chips.

4 Line a 23 x 23 cm (9 x 9 inch) baking tray with baking paper and pour in your rice pop mixture. It's very sticky, so scrape it in using a silicone spoon or spatula. Now wet your hands and use them to push down the mix in an even layer.

5 Place the milk chocolate pieces in a heatproof bowl and melt in the microwave – about 90 seconds on full power, but check after one minute. Drizzle it over the rice pop mixture in whatever way you like, then dot with your mini marshmallows and sprinkle with the sea salt flakes. Place in the fridge for at least 15 minutes. Once set, cut into 25 squares and serve.

Megan's don't mug me off cake

If you love chocolate cake but don't have time to make one, this is a quick and easy mug cake that is honestly sooo good. It comes out of the microwave nice and fluffy, looking pretty impressive, so I hope you enjoy.

SERVES 1

1 egg

2 tablespoons caster sugar

1 tablespoon vegetable oil

1 heaped tablespoon gluten-free self-raising flour

1 tablespoon cocoa powder

1 heaped tablespoon gluten-free chocolate spread

2–3 tablespoons milk, of your choice

1 Whisk your egg in a mug, then add your sugar and oil and whisk to combine.

2 Add your flour and cocoa powder and whisk again.

3 Now whisk in your chocolate spread and 2 tablespoons of milk until you have a thick, lump-free mixture. You might need to add a little more milk.

4 If you want your cake to be gooey in the middle, place it in the microwave for about 90 seconds on the highest setting. If you prefer your cake to be drier, cook it for about 2 minutes 10 seconds. The exact time depends on your microwave, so poke a knife into the cake to check its texture. If the blade comes out too sticky for your liking, continue to cook for a further few seconds.

Sparkling lemon posset

I love lemon-flavoured desserts, and this one is so easy but impressive. The zinginess of the lemons mixed in with the cream goes so well with the Dipping Shortbreads (see opposite). And there's nothing like edible glitter for a touch of glamour.

SERVES 4

600 ml (20 fl oz) double cream

200 g (7 oz) golden caster sugar

zest of 3 lemons, plus 5 tablespoons of the juice

edible glitter, to serve

1 Place your cream and sugar in a pan over a gentle heat and stir constantly, until the sugar has dissolved. At that point, increase the heat and allow the mixture to bubble for a few seconds. Remove from the heat, then stir in your lemon zest and juice.

2 Pour the posset into 4 cups or glasses. Set aside to cool to room temperature, then place in the fridge for 4 hours.

3 Before serving, dust the possets with your edible glitter.

Dipping shortbreads

With only four ingredients, this recipe is so easy to make. It's perfect for dipping in your Sparkling Lemon Possets (see opposite) and great with a cup of tea.

SERVES 4

110 g (3¾ oz) baking spread (I like Stork)

60 g (2¼ oz) caster sugar, plus extra for dusting

110 g (3¾ oz) gluten-free plain flour

50 g (1¾ oz) cornflour

1 Preheat your oven to 160°C/140°C fan (325°F)/Gas Mark 3. Set out a sheet of nonstick baking paper.

2 Place your baking spread and sugar in a bowl and beat together with a wooden spoon.

3 Sift in both your flours and stir until a crumbly mixture forms. Use your hands to knead the dough until smooth, then shape into a ball.

4 Sprinkle some extra caster sugar over your baking paper and place the dough in the middle. Using a rolling pin, roll it out to a thickness of about 5 mm (¼ inch).

5 Using a sharp knife or cookie cutter, cut your dough into fingers, circles or whatever shape you like. Reroll the offcuts and cut out as many more as you can.

6 Slide the baking paper and shortbread shapes onto a large baking sheet. Sprinkle with some more caster sugar and bake for 15–20 minutes, until lightly browned.

Mini egg brownies

I really do believe these are the best GF brownies around. I've tried many versions over the years and these are the most gooey and delicious. Also they're topped with mini eggs: you can't go wrong.

MAKES 12

170 g (6 oz) unsalted butter, at room temperature, cubed

200 g (7 oz) caster sugar

90 g (3¼ oz) brown sugar

3 large eggs

1 teaspoon vanilla extract

3 tablespoons gluten-free chocolate and hazelnut spread

70 g (2½ oz) gluten-free self-raising flour

40 g (1½ oz) cocoa powder

2 x 160 g (2¼ oz) packets mini chocolate eggs with a sugar shell

(3½ oz) milk chocolate, broken into pieces

cream or ice cream, to serve (optional)

1 Preheat your oven to 180°C/160°C fan (350°F)/Gas Mark 4. Line the bottom and sides of a deep baking tray, about 30 x 20 cm (12 x 8 inches), with non-stick baking paper.

2 Place your butter in a large bowl, add your sugars and whisk together until smooth and creamy.

3 Whisk in your eggs one at a time, then whisk in your vanilla extract and chocolate spread.

4 Sift your flour and cocoa powder into the butter bowl and fold in with a spoon until completely combined, with no spots of flour.

5 Finally, crush 1 bag of mini eggs and add to your batter.

6 Pour your brownie mix into the prepared tray and smooth the top.

7 Bake for 30 minutes, then lower the oven temperature to 160°C/140°C fan (325°F)/Gas Mark 3 and bake for another 20 minutes. Set aside to cool for 10 minutes.

8 In the meantime, roughly chop the remaining mini eggs and set aside. Place the milk chocolate pieces in a heatproof bowl and melt in the microwave – about 90 seconds on full power, but check after 1 minute. Drizzle it over the brownies, then sprinkle with the chopped mini eggs before the milk chocolate cools and sets.

Lemon sorbet loaded bowl

This dessert may sound strange to some people, but it's something I've eaten since I was little. The saltiness of the peanuts works so well with the lemon sorbet and the strawberry sauce. It's like bringing the ice cream van back to your home.

SERVES 2

6 large scoops of lemon sorbet

ready-made strawberry sauce

80 g (3 oz) salted peanuts, crushed

2 large chocolate flakes, each cut in half across the middle

1 Scoop your sorbet into 2 dessert bowls, then cover with your strawberry sauce.

2 Sprinkle your peanuts all over the top.

3 Crumble one half of a flake over each bowl. Stick the remaining halves into the sorbet and use them as spoons!

Sweet & salty chocolate-covered nachos

I love sweet and salty combos, so this recipe really hits the spot. Dip and enjoy!

SERVES 2

170 g (6 oz) bag of salted tortilla chips

4 handfuls of mini marshmallows

4 tablespoons chocolate chips

100 g (3½ oz) cream cheese

1 teaspoon vanilla extract

2 tablespoons runny honey

5 strawberries, finely chopped (as in a salsa)

½ lemon

ready-made chocolate sauce

90 g (3 oz) white chocolate

1 tablespoon icing sugar

1 Preheat your oven to 160°C/140°C fan (325°F)/ Gas Mark 3. Line a flat baking tray – I use a small one, about 25 x 18 cm (10 x 7 inches) but any size is fine – with non stick baking paper.

2 Arrange your nachos in the prepared tray, then sprinkle with your marshmallows and chocolate chips. Place in the oven until the top of the marshmallows has melted, about 10 minutes, but keep checking on it.

3 Meanwhile, place your cream cheese in a bowl. Add your vanilla extract and 1 tablespoon of the honey and whisk together. Spoon into 2 separate dipping pots.

4 Place your strawberries in another bowl, add a squeeze of lemon juice and the remaining tablespoon of honey. Mix together, then spoon into 2 more dipping pots.

5 Slide your chocolatey nachos off the baking paper and onto a serving tray or platter. Add your mini dipping pots around the sides.

6 Drizzle your chocolate sauce over the nachos, then grate your white chocolate on top. Place your icing sugar in a fine sieve or tea strainer and sprinkle over the tray. Tuck in!

Rhubarb crumble

I grew up eating crumbles, because my family grew our own fruit and veg, so this really takes me back to my childhood. You can serve this with cream, custard or ice cream.

SERVES 4

500 g (1 lb 2 oz) rhubarb, chopped into thumb-sized pieces

200 g (7 oz) caster sugar

½ lemon

For the crumble

175 g (6 oz) gluten-free plain flour

140 g (5 oz) caster sugar

140 g (5 oz) cold butter, cubed

½ teaspoon salt

1 teaspoon vanilla extract

100 g (3½ oz) gluten-free oats

1 Preheat your oven to 180°C/160°C fan (350°F)/ Gas Mark 4.

2 Place your rhubarb in a large frying pan over a low heat. Add half the caster sugar and warm for 15 minutes until the rhubarb has softened but it still holding its shape, and the sugar has dissolved. Taste and add more sugar if you want. When that has dissolved too, set the pan aside.

3 To make the crumble, put your flour into a large bowl. Add your sugar, butter and salt, then rub together with your fingers, until the mix resembles breadcrumbs. Add your vanilla extract, then mix in your oats.

4 Transfer your rhubarb to a baking dish, about 20 x 20 cm (8 x 8 inches). Squeeze a drizzle of lemon juice over it, then sprinkle lightly with some of the remaining caster sugar. Spoon your crumble on top so the surface is completely covered. Add another sprinkle of sugar, but only if you have some left over from the rhubarb.

5 Bake for 35–40 minutes, until golden brown!

It's always a sad moment
when you get offered ice
cream in a restaurant...
I want a brownie, I want a
crumble. Let a gluten-free
girl live, please!

————————

Maybe some restaurants will
get my book and add some
of the dishes to the menu!
A girl can dream, right?

———————————

At least we can end this book on
a sweet note and share our love
for sugar together!

INDEX

UK/US GLOSSARY

apple cider	hard cider	jug	pitcher
baking beans	pie weights	pepper	bell pepper
caster sugar	superfine sugar	piping bag	pastry bag
clingfilm	plastic wrap	plain flour	all-purpose flour
coriander leaves	cilantro	rocket	arugula
cornflour	cornstarch	red/yellow pepper	bell pepper
double cream	heavy cream	self-raising flour	self-rising flour
flaked almonds	slivered almonds	spring onions	scallions
foil	aluminum foil	stock cube	bouillon cube
icing sugar	confectioners' sugar	takeaway	takeout

ACKNOWLEDGEMENTS

Jade Reuben, my manager and publicist – thank you for being by my side always and for believing in me to create a second cookbook. Also thank you for spending a year going back and forth with messages and photos to make this book the best it can be. We really are the dream team and you're the best critic when it comes to food tasting! I always trust your guidance.

Jo Bell – I couldn't ask for a better book agent and have loved working with you these last few years. Thank you for being so kind and helpful throughout this whole process, spending hours on Zoom calls with me making sure everything's perfect. You make everything so calm and easy, I love the way you work. Thank you for everything.

Kate Fox – thank you for all your time and hard work making this the best gluten-free book on the market. I love how much passion you have for this book and I couldn't be more grateful. And Natalie Bradley – thank you so much for all your work, it really means so much. Alex Stetter – thank you working with my crazy ideas and for all the long days on the shoots.

Erin Brown and Megan Brown – thank you so much for all the time, work and effort you have put into getting the marketing and publicity campaigns for the book just right, I appreciate everything you do.

Jaz Bahra and Nicky Collings – thank you both so much for everything. You make this whole process so much fun and I love working with both of you on shoot days! Jaz, I'm so happy we got to do another book together, and Nicky, I've loved getting to work with you on this book. You're both so lovely and warm, and I hope we can work together again.

Luke Albert – thank you for bringing my vision to life. Your photography is insane and I'm very lucky that I got to work with you on something so special to me. The photos really make this book! It looks exactly how I imagined and I'm so grateful for all your time and attention to detail on every single dish.

Anna Wilkins – thank you for every single bit of detailing you put into the prop styling for this book. You are a perfectionist like me and it was a dream to work with you. Your visions for the photo shoot were just as I had imagined and hopefully we can work together again in the future. Thank you for all the time you put into the long shoot days!

Sam Dixon – thank you so much for EVERYTHING. You made every dish look incredible and I loved working with you in the kitchen. Thank you for putting up with me. I appreciate all your time and effort to making sure the book was 10 out of 10. It was lovely to share being pregnant together on the shoot, too.

Allegra D'Agostini, Lucy Turnbull, Eden Owen-Jones – thank you all for being the best assistant chefs. I couldn't have asked for three more lovely people, who all knew exactly what was best for the book. What a team!

And thank you to Patricia Burgess, Lucy Bannell and Cathy Heath, and to production controllers Lucy Carter and Nic Jones. There wouldn't be a book without you all.

Jade, Kate, Jackie, Joe, Felan and Martin at Bold Management – thank you for being the best team! I have loved working with you for all these years.

Ellis Ranson – thank you for styling me just perfectly. When it comes to clothes, you always know what's best. I love working with you and had so much fun on the shoot. The vibes were on point! Rowan Ireland – thank you for creating the big hair that I envisioned and making me look beautiful. You really brought the glam, every photo looks incredible.

Milly McKenna – thank you for always being my cooking bestie and especially for helping me with my sweet treats. You really are an amazing chef and I'm lucky you're my sister, so we can enjoy the food together!

Mum – thank you for everything, for your help and all your family traditions and the recipes that we grew up with. If it wasn't for you, I wouldn't be the chef I am today. I'm so lucky to have a mum like you.

Nan – thank you for always being my number one fan and food critic. If it wasn't for Granddad, none of us would be able to cook. We all learned from the best.

Oli – thank you for being the best food taster there is and for making me fall in love with you even more by supporting me through my cooking journey. Also for being the best helper in the kitchen with the pots and pans. I promise I'll try to get better with the mess. Haha. I love you.

My darling Landon – you make the whole world better and I can't wait for you to try my yummy dinners. It's going to be a fun few years working out what you enjoy and, at some point, cooking together. We love you so much.

ABOUT MEGAN

Megan McKenna is a TV personality, highly engaged influencer and brand ambassador, with social media platforms totalling over 4.5 million followers. She is an ambassador for the Natasha Allergy Research Foundation and has also become a campaigner for coeliac disease and wheat allergies, and she has presented segments on allergies for various TV shows, including *The One Show*.

Having started her career making appearances on MTV and ITV shows, she had her own three-part TV series, *There's Something About Megan*, and went on to release a country music album and regular single releases too.

Megan penned the *Sunday Times* bestselling book *Mouthy* and went on to be crowned *The X Factor: Celebrity* winner in 2019. A passionate home cook, she was a finalist on *Celebrity Master Chef* and her first cookbook, *Can You Make That Gluten-Free?*, was published in 2022.